Ministry of Education, Ontario
Information Services
13th Floor, Mowat Block, Queen's Park
Toronto   M7A 1L2

Activities for Trainers:
50 Useful Designs

Activities for Trainers:
50 Useful Designs

**by
Cyril R. Mill**

**University Associates
8517 Production Avenue
San Diego, California 92121**

Copyright © 1980 by University Associates, Inc.
ISBN: 088390-159-5
Library of Congress Catalog Card Number: 80-50465
Printed in the United States of America

The materials that appear in this book (except those for which reprint permission must be obtained from the primary sources) may be freely reproduced for educational/training activities. There is no requirement to obtain special permission for such uses. We do, however, ask that the following statement appear on all reproductions:

Reproduced from
Activities for Trainers:
50 Useful Designs
Cyril R. Mill
San Diego, California: University Associates, Inc., 1980

This permission statement is limited to reproduction of materials for educational or training events. *Systematic or large-scale reproduction or distribution – or inclusion of items in publications for sale – may be done only with prior written permission.*

Contents

Preface ... vii
Introduction ... ix

Part 1. Group Dynamics and Laboratory Training
1. Introduction to Group Dynamics ... 3
2. Clear and Unclear Goals ... 5
3. Leadership and Maintenance Functions ... 9
4. The Numbers Game ... 14
5. Categories ... 17
6. Ability to Follow Directions ... 20
7. Internal Dialogue ... 22
8. The Fishbowl ... 25
9. Tinkertoys ... 29
10. Marathon ... 31
11. Structural Interventions ... 33
12. Conference Techniques ... 35
13. Values: Influencing Others ... 39
14. Situational Leadership ... 43
15. Checking Out Nonverbal Communication ... 48
16. Dream Collection ... 50
17. A Nature Walk ... 52
18. A Nonverbal "Who Am I?" Experience ... 54
19. Whole-Brain Function ... 56
20. Practice in Saying "No" ... 60
21. The Relationship Contraption ... 62

Part 2. The Training of Trainers
22. A Guide for Designing a Training Program ... 69
23. A Memory Bank for Facilitators ... 72
24. Sample Guides for Group Observation and Evaluation ... 76
25. Training Group Discussion Leaders ... 94

Part 3. Cross-Cultural Training
26. A Cross-Cultural Experience ... 103
27. Intergroup Collaboration: A Cross-Cultural Experience ... 109

Part 4. Stress Training

28.	Stress: A Mental Arithmetic Experiment	115
29.	Develop Your Support System	117
30.	A Stress-Management Program	121
31.	Type A and Type B: Check List	124

Part 5. Women's Issues

32.	The Pre-Employment Interview	129
33.	Promoting Women	137
34.	Sexism: Discussion Topics	141
35.	Presenting Yourself: Skill Training for Women	147
36.	Career Planning for Women	156

Part 6. Supervisory Training

37.	Supervisory Training: A Workshop Opener	175
38.	Supervisory Training: Role Clarification	180
39.	House of Cards	185
40.	Giving Orders	188

Part 7. The Training of Consultants

41.	Consultant's Check List for Initial Client Contact	195
42.	Consultant Skills: Interviewing	196
43.	Consultation Skills: Planning the Next Visit	203

Part 8. Management and Organization Development

44.	Introduction to Organization Diagnosis	209
45.	Win/Lose Competition	213
46.	Volunteering	217
47.	Seven Questions	219
48.	Decision Making: An Unexpected Activity	221
49.	Team Building: Disposing of the Past	223
50.	Team Building	225

Preface

On a recent holiday, I was once again reminded of the vivid, lasting impression left by experiential learning. When a man at our dining table heard that I am a trainer and consultant, he eagerly recounted memories of a role-playing skit in which he had been a participant. He identified the roles assigned to all eight members of his group and not only recalled the excitement of the activity, but displayed such verve in his voice, expression, and gestures that he was obviously reliving the experience. I asked him when he had participated in the training program. It was ten years ago! We could not help but comment on the efficacy of a method of learning that enables the learner to reproduce such detail after the passage of so much time.

The collection of resource material in this book has been prepared as my contribution toward fostering the continuation and expansion of experiential learning. When I first began to conduct group training programs, I took great comfort in developing my own resource file. In 1954, I was still learning how to make a point without resorting to lecture. Each time some new idea worked, I stored it away, hoping to be able to use it again. Today my collection of files of activities and theory-session ideas fills several drawers. I have come to terms with the paradox that I know more than I can recall, and much of what I know is in those file drawers. Going through them before embarking on a new training or consulting assignment stimulates and prepares me for meeting the group needs I expect to encounter.

Many of my colleagues must have a similar collection back home. Often, during a planning session, one of them will say, "I think I have that here," and, rummaging around in a briefcase full of material, will come up with just what we need.

This book is like a filing cabinet: a set of materials selected and refined to meet a variety of training needs. Although the book began as a revision of two earlier publications, *20 Exercises for Trainers* and *20 Exercises for the Classroom*, the idea of a mere revision was soon dropped after re-reading those materials. Some of the basic concepts in group dynamics have held up over the ten years since their first publication, but many of the activities designed to demonstrate the concepts now seem time-worn or trivial. This condition compelled me to undertake a major revision of those that still hold value and to add others that represent the social concerns encountered by today's trainers and consultants.

The application of laboratory training has undergone considerable change since 1972 when *20 Exercises for Trainers* and *20 Exercises for the Classroom* were published. There are fewer demands today for human relations or T-group training. However, there is a continuing demand for training that uses experiential methods while focusing on a skill, attitude, or area of knowledge that is of use in the management of organizations. The collection of activities in this book reflects this change and is, therefore, a major revision of the earlier publications. There are fewer activities related to basic laboratory methods and basic communications skills and more activities designed for use with women in management, coping with stress, and cross-cultural training; and there are more interventions of use in the training and practice of organizational consultants.

I have no doubt that ten years from now, or even sooner, another edition of this book will be needed. Given the rapid development in our understanding of ourselves and the changes that will take place in society, the book will probably again have to contain new activities rather than a revision of the old. In the meantime, it is hoped that this set of resources will be used with enjoyment to provide enduring growth and memorable experiences for group participants.

I cannot sufficiently express my appreciation to the many consultants, trainers, and trainees with whom I have worked over the years. There are too many to name, but I want to take this opportunity to give them my thanks and to say that I have learned much from them. I hope the activities in this collection will, to a small extent, offer them something in return.

Vienna, Virginia　　　　　　　　　　　　　　　　　　　　　　　　　　　　Cyril R. Mill
1980

AUTHORSHIP AND PRINTING HISTORY

Authorship and origin of many of the ideas that are basic to these activities cannot be definitely attributed. When authorship is known, credit is given in footnotes. Sixteen of the activities first appeared in two 1972 packets published by NTL Learning Resources Corporation. These activities are listed under the title of the original publication, as follows:

Twenty Exercises for the Classroom

　　The Fishbowl

Twenty Exercises for Trainers

　　Clear and Unclear Goals
　　Categories
　　Ability to Follow Directions
　　Internal Dialogue
　　Tinkertoys
　　Marathon
　　Structural Interventions
　　Dream Collection
　　A Nonverbal "Who Am I?" Experience
　　Practice in Saying "No"
　　The Relationship Contraption
　　Win/Lose Competition
　　Volunteering
　　Seven Questions
　　Team Building

Introduction

This set of resources will be valuable to many audiences. First of all, it is addressed to experienced trainers or facilitators and to organizational consultants. It should also be useful in college courses in group dynamics and organizational behavior. Many training divisions in government agencies and industrial organizations will find useful material here for their work. Persons who plan conferences and design large meetings will find valuable tips, e.g., chapter 25, "Training Group Discussion Leaders." Group therapists may discover methods for enhancing their work with groups that were not included in their formal training courses.

The user of these materials is cautioned not to set aside lightly those activities with familiar names: All of them have been altered or given a new twist. This is particularly true in the first section, Group Dynamics and Laboratory Training. Where it seemed useful, observers' guides or self-diagnostic check lists have been added. Although the procedures of administering an activity may be changed, acknowledgement is given to the original creator of the idea wherever that person is known.

Experienced trainers will find part 2, "The Training of Trainers," of value, particularly "A Memory Bank for Facilitators." Many of us live in two worlds — in our everyday jobs on a campus or in the corporate world, and in the occasional world of laboratory education, where we try to practice a more ideal set of values and behaviors. It would be comforting if the two worlds fit together better than they do, but since there is slippage, we need an instrument such as the memory bank to help us shift into performing facilitation as we know it should be.

The activities of part 3, "Cross-Cultural Training" can be useful to individuals concerned with intercultural relationships such as in campus training programs for foreign students, in the training of foreign-service personnel in industry or government, or in work with subcultures in our own country. Too often, such training degenerates into sterile briefings on manners, customs, or "how to do business in Patawami." The idea of constructing artificial cultures keeps the general intercultural dynamics in clear view and helps the trainee to focus on his or her own culture and the difficulties of viewing the world from a different perspective.

No section of activities is intended to be definitive or all encompassing in a particular topical area. The activities are offered rather as possible additions to the skilled trainer's present set of resources. For instance, the four activities in part 4, "Stress Training," may be of use to consultants engaged in helping an organization to deal with this problem. However, they do not in themselves constitute a complete stress-management training program. Incidentally, "Type A and Type B: Check List" may be an especially useful alternative to the traditional lecture on the topic of coronary risk.

The range of content in this collection is quite broad, reflecting many aspects of the current social scene. Part 5, for instance, focuses on women's issues and one of these, "Career Planning for Women," is a four-session course to be conducted over a month's time.

In part 6, only the first activity, "Supervisory Training: A Workshop Opener," is strictly directed toward supervisors. The other three activities have been used in supervisory training programs but would serve equally well for management training at higher levels. Many people who are in charge of the work of others have difficulty with a very basic skill — how to give orders. Activity 40 addresses this problem in a way that builds skill in giving orders while simultaneously presenting a scale of styles, easily recalled the next time the skill is called for on the job.

Training programs for consultants often emphasize the initial phases such as entering a relationship with a client, doing a diagnosis, and team building. Little is said about what a consultant should do on the fifth or the twelfth visit. How does a consultant maintain a relationship over a long time and develop a sequential, consistently helpful style? What are the ethics of selling the client more than he initially bargained for? Activity 43, "Consultation Skills: Planning the Next Visit," goes directly into these issues. Also in part 7, the activity on interviewing skills has been productive in work with others, besides consultants, who regularly engage in interviewing, such as social workers and psychologists who conduct therapy sessions and managers who conduct performance appraisal interviews.

The activities in part 8 are appropriate interventions when an organizational consultant is working with intact management groups such as during an off-site team building session. A not-infrequent phenomenon is taken up in activity 49, "Team Building: Disposing of the Past." When there is a need to mourn for the past, and to bring the old guard and the newcomers together, this activity is recommended. The final team building activity, chapter 50, is almost fail-safe. Several of my colleagues have used it with success, saying that it develops a feeling among people of being members of a close-knit group in a very short time.

It is assumed that the users of these activities will have sufficient skill to deal in a professional manner with the group phenomena and the individual reactions that are produced. This implies a behavioral science background, participation in previous laboratories as a learner and as a trainer, and acquaintance with the democratic and humanitarian values that are essential to the constructive use of experiential learning.

Part one
Group Dynamics and Laboratory Training

1 Introduction to Group Dynamics

Purposes

I. To introduce group members to the vocabulary and concepts of group dynamics.

II. To enable members to diagnose behavior in terms of group phenomena.

Group Size

This session can be conducted as a lecture or seminar and is suitable for a group of ten to thirty persons.

Time Required

One hour.

Materials

A blank flipchart and markers.

Procedure

I. Introduce this lecture with the following comments:

Most people think of behavior as determined by personal characteristics, habit, and experience. Some people attribute behavior of individuals to psychoanalytic principles such as defense systems, childhood rearing, or even transference. Whatever its cause, human behavior is unpredictable unless you know a great deal about the individuals involved.

However, when people gather together to work as a group, group dynamics come into play which, if you know and understand them, make the behavior of the people in the group more comprehensible and sometimes even more predictable.

I want to present a scheme of some of these group dynamics so that you can remember them and begin to use them. As members of a group, we are continually acting at two levels: participating and observing. Knowing about group dynamics will help us to become better observers and will help us to diagnose what is going on so that we can become more sophisticated in our participation.

II. Draw Figure 1 on the flipchart.

As you draw the diagram, explain it and give the following names to each element:

1. Number 1, the circle, represents the group.
2. Number 2, the square, represents the goal toward which the group is working.
3. Number 3, the arrow, represents the path toward the goal or how the group is going to achieve the goal.
4. Number 4 represents the life space or the environment in which the group

exists—the company, school, organization, or community of which the group is a part.

5. Number 5 represents another group nearby, which may be working toward the same goal or even toward a different goal.

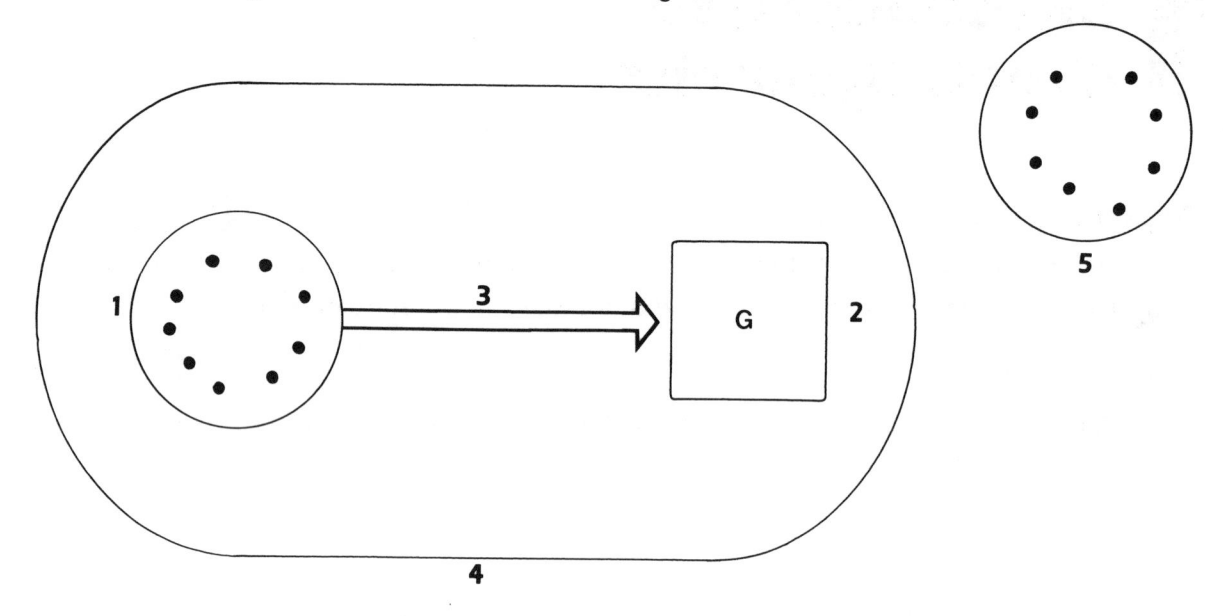

Figure 1. Group dynamics

III. Continue the lecture, covering the following information:

There are characteristics of each of these elements of group dynamics that predictably will come into play in a group and have an effect on the behavior of the members. These characteristics are very different from the intra-psychic characteristics to which we usually attribute behavior. If we are to become skilled group observers and participants, it will help us to think in terms of group dynamics, such as the following:

1. *Dynamics of the group:* Functions of leadership and of maintenance, amount of participation, decision-making style, climate, status, size of the group, life span of the group.
2. *Dynamics of the goal:* Its clarity, acceptability to the group, attainability, distance in time, attractiveness, importance.
3. *Dynamics of the path of the goal:* The use of the problem-solving process, alternative solutions, available resources, choice points, subgoals for increasing motivation, moral acceptability of means.
4. *Dynamics of the environment:* Its support or repression of the group and its goals, stability or instability, provision of needed resources.
5. *Intergroup dynamics:* Communication problems, stereotyping, competition or collaboration, trust, territoriality.

IV. At your discretion, the lecture may be enriched by illustrations from your experience or from the group life of the members to whom the lecture is addressed.

V. In order to demonstrate the reality of these group dynamics, immediately follow the lecture with "Clear and Unclear Goals," activity 2 in this book.

2 Clear and Unclear Goals

Purposes

I. To demonstrate the contrasting consequences on group behavior and climate of having clear goals and unclear goals.

II. To generalize from this learning experience to back-home applications in staff or committee work.

Group Size

All members of a training group participate in this activity. Participants work in groups of six to eight each, with an observer for each group.

Time Required

One hour.

Setting

Each group works in a circle, seated around a table (if available).

Materials

I. A copy of the Observation Guide and a pencil for each participant.

II. A blank flipchart and markers.

III. The two tasks written on the flipchart, ready to be exposed one at a time at the appropriate moment.

Procedure

I. Announce that this demonstration illustrates the influence of a group dynamic on how a group works together. Do *not* mention that the group dynamic is goal clarity.

II. Ask that each group select an observer and then get acquainted while the observers receive their briefing. Collect the observers together and give them enough copies of the Observation Guide for themselves and for members of their groups. Tell them that the groups will be given two tasks. The statement of the first task will be unclear, the statement of the second task will be clear. The observer's job is to record careful observations of the group's behavior during the performance of the two tasks. The members will not be given copies of the Observation Guide until the tasks are completed and it is time for analysis of the data.

III. Tell the observers to return to their respective groups but to sit outside the circle of members.

IV. Brief all groups as follows:

> We are going to study group behavior by working on two brief tasks. Your observer will not participate but will report to you at the end of the second task. Your task will take about eight minutes. I will give you a warning a minute before the time is up. Here is the problem for you to discuss.

Expose the following question, written on the flipchart ahead of time.

Task A
> What are the most appropriate goals to govern the best development group experiences in order to maximize social development in a democratic society?

V. The groups work on the task and the observers take notes. Give a warning at seven minutes; at eight minutes, tell the participants to stop the discussion.

VI. Expose the following statement of the second task:

Task B
> List as many as you can of the formally organized clubs or organizations that exist in a typical community.

VII. The groups work on the second task, and the observers take notes. Warn the groups at five minutes and stop their discussion at six minutes.

Analysis of the Data

I. Each observer gives a blank copy of the Observation Guide to each participant in his or her group and reports his or her observations to the group.

II. After you explain that the purpose of the discussion is not for the members to agree or disagree with the observer but to share their perceptions more generally, each group discusses the observations.

Facilitator Presents Brief Theory

I. After the observers have made their reports to their groups (about ten minutes), stop the discussion and ask the following questions:

   A. In general, what were the differences in behavior for Tasks A and B?
   B. Was the nature of the task the primary cause of these differences?
   C. Did your feelings differ during the two tasks?
   D. How would you describe each of the two tasks?

II. Use the flipchart to present the following information:

Characteristics of well-formulated group goals are:
- Clarity
- Acceptability to the group
- Attainability
- Openness to modification or clarification

The agenda for any group meeting should have these same characteristics. Agenda items are group goals, which the group can then take up one by one.

In a staff meeting or committee meeting, indications that the group's goals are unclear or unacceptable to many members can include the following:
- Tension, joking, or horseplay
- Deflection of discussion to side issues
- Failure to use, support, or build on worthy ideas

Generalization

I. Ask the groups to reform and to discuss application of these principles to back-home groups. Elicit or provide examples that illustrate (1) an agenda (group goals) that is clear, publicly shared, and open to modification; and (2) one that is not. Ask, "What are the consequences in the behavior and the climate in those groups?"

OBSERVATION GUIDE

	First Task	Second Task
1. Number of times the goal was clarified or asked to be clarified.		
2. Assessment of "working climate" in the group. Was it cooperative, hostile, pleasant, critical, accepting, etc.? At the beginning		
At the middle		
At the end		
3. Verbal behavior not directly related to getting the job done (side conversation, jokes, comments).		
4. Nonverbal behavior not related to getting the task done (looking around the room, horseplay, bored withdrawal, hostility).		
5. How much progress did the group make in getting the task done? (Make an estimate.)		

3 Leadership and Maintenance Functions

Purposes

I. To identify behaviors that meet individual needs and group needs so that group goals can be met.

II. To demonstrate the use of selected functions in meeting individual and group needs.

Group Size

The demonstration requires nine people; the remaining group members become the audience, which may be any size.

Time Required

One hour.

Setting

A room is needed that is large enough for a circle of nine chairs to be placed in the center for the demonstration participants and for the other group members to be seated around the outside of the circle, similar to a theater in the round.

Materials

I. An Instruction Slip for each of the nine participants in the demonstration.

II. A copy of the Group Functions and Role Chart and a pencil for every group member.

Procedure

I. Provide a context for the activity by giving the following information:

   A. Every group has a job to do.
      1. Even a social group has a task, that is, to assure that people enjoy themselves by entering into a conversation and by listening.
      2. Most groups, such as a committee, a staff meeting, or a task force, have clearly defined goals.

   B. Most people develop habits of group participation, and some of these habits serve to help or hinder a group from getting its job done.

   C. We are going to demonstrate a group at work in a way that will help us to see some of the habits or functions that are typically present in the group. We'll need nine people for the demonstration and the rest of us will watch.

II. Select nine persons to take seats in the center circle, and give each of them an Instruction Slip. Announce to the audience:

   Each of our demonstrators is being asked to participate in this meeting in only one way. This will make for an unusual group session, but it will help us to see some of the behaviors that help or hinder a group from getting its job done.

III. Describe the situation:

This group is a policy committee appointed by a liberal church to make a recommendation on the position that the church should take on an important issue. The committee members are used to discussing things together, and they listen well to one another. At this point, they want to come to a consensus on their policy recommendation. The issue for which the committee is to make a recommendation is this: Is there a new sexual morality in society today that the church should take a stand on?

IV. Allow the committee to discuss the issue for about eight minutes. When the time is up, ask the demonstrators to leave their Instruction Slips on their chairs and move two seats to the right. Tell them to read the Instruction Slip left on their new seats and to continue with the discussion. However, this time, each committee member performs a different function.

V. After eight minutes, ask the demonstrators to move two more seats to the right and to continue the discussion by performing in terms of the role described by the Instruction Slip for that chair.

VI. Stop the discussion after another five minutes and ask the demonstrators to remain where they are.
   A. Ask the audience to identify the various functions that were associated with the nine chairs of the demonstration.
   B. Ask the demonstrators to identify which functions they found easy or difficult to perform.
   C. Focus discussion on the roles of the Blocker and the Self-Seeker (Boaster) to underline the fact that the presence of these two roles hindered the group.
   D. Thank the demonstrators and allow them to return to their seats with the audience.

VII. Hand out to each participant a copy of the Group Functions and Roles Chart and a pencil.
   A. Review this chart to indicate that *functions* differ from *roles:*
      1. *Functions* are divided into those behaviors that help a group to get its job done (Task) and those that help to hold the group together (Maintenance). They are called "functions" because they are behaviors that anyone can perform.
      2. *Roles* refers to behaviors that are closely tied to individual styles or personalities. Sometimes these are habits that can be changed through training or feedback.
   B. At the next meeting of this group (T-group or other kinds of groups that may be used in a training program), this form may be used to identify who is performing what kinds of functions in the group.
   C. It is important to learn to avoid playing an individual role in a group, and, instead, learn to perform as many of the task and maintenance functions as are necessary to help the group.

INSTRUCTION SLIPS

Facilitator Instructions: The following nine Instruction Slips are to be typed or copied and cut so that one function can be given to each demonstrator. Note that there are four Task Functions: **Give Information, Seek Information and Ask Questions, Clarify or Elaborate,** and **Summarize.** There are three Maintenance Functions: **Encouraging Others, Harmonizing,** and **Gatekeeping.** And there are two Individual Roles: the **Blocker** and the **Self-Seeker or Boaster.**

Your function is to **Give Information.** You may provide facts (even if you must make them up), state your beliefs, and give any suggestions of ideas that come to mind.

Your function is to **Seek Information** and **Ask Questions.** You may request facts relevant to the group concern, ask for suggestions and ideas, and draw out the opinions of others.

Your function is to **Clarify** or **Elaborate.** You will help to clear up confusion by interpreting what others have said, give examples that illustrate the issue, and restate in your own words the opinions expressed by others.

Your function is to **Summarize.** This can be done at any time (do not wait until the end). You try to pull together related ideas, you reflect what the group seems to be agreeing or disagreeing on, or test for consensus by offering a decision based on what others have said.

Your function is to **Encourage Others** by being friendly, warm, and responsive to them. You show that you accept them and their contributions.

Your function is to **Harmonize** by attempting to reconcile disagreements. Find areas of commonality and point them out. Reduce tension by getting people to explore their differences.

Your function is **Gatekeeping**. Make sure that everyone who wants a chance to talk gets an opportunity. For instance, say, "Let's hear from _____. He has been wanting to say something." You can also suggest ways the group can work better together.

Your role is the **Blocker**. Show that you think differently than the rest of the group. When agreement is nearly reached, voice an opposite point of view. You can slow up the group by reviewing something already settled or stop the group by taking an unreasonable stand.

Your role is the **Self-Seeker** or **Boaster**. Indicate that you know all about the topic and have already done anything that might be suggested. Volunteer to take leadership or do other things to push yourself forward.

GROUP FUNCTIONS AND ROLES CHART

NAMES OF GROUP MEMBERS

TASK FUNCTIONS	Initiating: gives ideas, proposes a task
	Seeking information: asks for facts, ideas
	Giving information: offers facts, ideas, beliefs
	Clarifying & elaborating: clears up confusion
	Summarizing: restates, offers a conclusion
	Consensus testing: checks on group position
MAINTENANCE FUNCTIONS	Harmonizing: reduces tension, explores differences
	Gatekeeping: facilitates participation of others
	Encouraging others: acts friendly, warm, accepting
	Compromising: yields status, admits error
	Standard setting: helps set norms, tests limits
INDIVIDUAL ROLES	Blocks: prevents consensus, movement
	Dominates: talks more than his/her fair share
	Plays: uses humor or jokes inappropriately
	Is self-seeking: oppresses with personal needs

Part 1. Group Dynamics and Laboratory Training

4 The Numbers Game

Purposes

I. To provide a quick demonstration of the variability in group members' ability to perceive patterns among complex data.
II. To illustrate the worth of such ability.
III. To break the ice — an interesting introduction to a group session.

Group Size

A minimum of seven or eight participants is required; the activity may also be used with a large group in a lecture room or an auditorium.

Time Required

About fifteen minutes.

Setting

This activity is useful at the beginning of a team-building session, especially if there is some anticipatory tension. It may also be used to provide an experiential break in a lecture presentation.

Procedure

I. Introduce the activity with the following:

> When a group of people is dealing with a set of complex issues, it takes a great deal of insight to bring all the data together in a way that makes sense. There is a short test that illustrates how information that is apparently random often is not as haphazard as it seems. Since it takes only a few minutes to do it, we will do it now and learn something about approaching complicated tasks.

II. Hand out the Numbers Game Sheet face down, asking participants not to look at it until everyone is ready.

III. When all the participants are ready, give directions as follows:

> I will be keeping time on this activity. Turn the page over and put your pencil on Number 1. Your task is to draw a line connecting all the numbers in turn. Draw a line to number 2. It is all right to cross lines. Raise your hand when you are finished. Now continue as fast as you can.

For a similar activity with different objectives, see "Numbers: A Problem-Solving Activity" by Brent D. Rubin and Richard W. Budd. In J. W. Pfeiffer and J. E. Jones (Eds.), *The 1978 Annual Handbook for Group Facilitators*. San Diego, CA: University Associates, 1978.

IV. Begin timing. Note the elapsed time when the first person finishes and also when the last one is through.
V. When all the participants are finished:
   A. Announce the completion times for the first and last persons.
   B. Ask if anyone perceived any order or pattern in the numbers. Display a Numbers Game Sheet and show the following pattern:
      1. Odd numbers are on the left.
      2. Even numbers are on the right.
      3. The pattern moves down the page, then up, then down again.
   C. Emphasize the fact that perceiving the pattern reduces the area to be examined and speeds up completion time — analyzing the structure of a task can increase efficiency.
VI. No further point need be made. With this introduction, you and the group can readily move into your agenda.

THE NUMBERS GAME SHEET

5 Categories

Purposes

I. To help workshop participants become initially acquainted with one another.

II. To provide a visually impressive demonstration of the differences in beliefs and values existing in a group.

Group Size

All persons in a workshop may participate — the more the better. This activity has worked successfully with groups of thirty, sixty, and one hundred persons.

Time Required

From thirty minutes to one hour.

Setting

A large room in which all the participants can move around.

Materials

I. Before the group assembles, prepare large sheets of paper as category posters. Hang four sets (or stacks) of the posters in the four corners of the room. The posters may be made in the following manner:

A. Select a few sets of contrasting terms that describe a category relevant to the training goals and the needs of the group. Examples of such categories may be found in the rows (left to right) of the Suggested Categories Sheet.

B. Using large sheets of newsprint, print four posters, each containing one of the terms describing a category. For example, the first four posters might read as follows:

| Inner City | Suburban | Rural | Other |

C. Print the next four posters (probably unrelated to the category of the first set of posters) and place them on top of the first set. This second set might read:

| Conservative | Militant | Liberal | Passive |

This activity was adapted from one developed by David Bork, 7236 Ridge Road, Frederick, Maryland 21701.

D. Continue printing and stacking (one poster on top of another) sets of category posters. Place a blank sheet over the top poster in each of the four stacks and hang a stack in each corner of the room.

Note: If this activity is used as a mixer, you may use as many as six or eight sets. If the purpose is to identify and remember individuals who take a certain stand on an issue, three or four sets is the maximum.

Procedure

I. Introduce the activity with comments that include the following ideas:
- As we look around at the group assembled here, we are naturally curious about one another.
- Superficial characteristics such as sex, age, and appearance are readily apparent, but more important in our working together will be our views on important issues, our attitudes, and our feelings.
- This activity can help us to identify individuals who share our views as well as those who look at issues differently from ourselves.
- Here are four terms with which we might describe ourselves.

II. Remove the blank sheets from the stack of posters in each corner, announcing the following instructions:

After looking at each of these four descriptions for a moment, go to the corner where the word or phrase is one that you would use in describing yourself. When you get there you will have about seven minutes to sit and talk with the others who are there with you. Talk about your reasons for choosing this description and how you feel about being with this group.

If anyone protests about the difficulty of identifying with any of the terms of a particular set, suggest that the person choose the least uncomfortable description and talk about it with the others who chose that term.

III. After seven minutes, remove this set of four sheets and expose the posters containing the next set of terms.

IV. Ask the members to repeat the procedure, again selecting the terms that they would use in describing *themselves* and regrouping for a seven-minute discussion.

V. Repeat for the remaining sets of terms.

SUGGESTED CATEGORIES SHEET

A	**B**	**C**	**D**
Black	White	Brown	Other
Liberal	Conservative	Passive	Militant
Tokenism	Racial balance	Desegregation	Segregation
✗ Action oriented	Move slowly	Go with majority	Do not get involved
✓ Learner	Helper	Teacher	Friend
Male	Androgynous	Female	Other
Lower class	Middle class	Upper class	Other
✗ Improve	Understand	Stabilize	Transcend
Prejudiced	Other	Unprejudiced	Racist
Republican	Independent	Democrat	Disinterested
Scotch	Bourbon	Tequila	Other
✗ Inner city	Suburban	Rural	Other
Catholic	Protestant	Jew	Other
Tall	Medium	Short	Other
Teachers	Counselors	Secretaries	Other
✗ Other	Line	Staff	Management
Shy	Friendly	Sophisticated	Other
Young	Older	Middle aged	Other
Colonial	Other	Contemporary	Traditional

Part 1. Group Dynamics and Laboratory Training   19

6 Ability to Follow Directions

Purposes

This "test" serves as an icebreaker and has little other purpose.

Group Size

Any number can participate because the test is taken individually.

Time Required

About fifteen minutes.

Setting

Participants can be seated in classroom or auditorium style.
Note: It is not recommended that this activity be used by a trainer with his own training group (T-group), because there is an element of trickery here that may run counter to the building of trust and confidence.

Materials

I. A copy of the Three-Minute Test and a pencil for each participant.

Procedure

I. Introduce the activity by saying, "We are going to take a test," and build up the idea of following a rigorous testing procedure:
- Check to see that everyone has a pencil.
- Suggest that the test results will be used in some way, such as forming work groups of people of equal ability.
- Make the test seem important by mentioning the difficulty of identifying leaders in a new group.
- Stress that although there is a five-minute limit, the "more capable people" will be finished in three minutes or less.
- Distribute the test face down, look at your watch, and give the sign to start the test.

II. When the time limit has passed (five minutes), allow the participants to talk about the experience a little, especially about their feelings of being tested and tricked. Center discussion on the following questions:
- What does the activity show about your ability to follow directions?
- Were competition and striving-for-achievement present as motivating factors?
- What feelings were aroused toward the tester?
- What is manipulation? Is it ethical to conceal information from others in order to achieve a learning goal for them?

THREE-MINUTE TEST

1. Read everything before doing anything.
2. Put your name in the upper-right-hand corner of the paper.
3. Circle the word **name** in the second sentence.
4. Draw five small squares in the upper-left-hand corner of this paper.
5. Put an **X** in each square mentioned in number 4.
6. Put a circle around each square.
7. Sign your name under the title of this page.
8. After the title, write **yes, yes, yes.**
9. Put a circle around the sentence number 7.
10. Put an **X** in the lower left-hand corner of this page.
11. Draw a triangle around the **X** you just made.
12. On the back of this page, multiply 70 x 30.
13. Draw a circle around the word **paper** in sentence number 4.
14. Loudly call out your first name when you get to this point in the test.
15. If you think that you have carefully followed directions, call out, "I have."
16. On the reverse side of this paper, add 107 and 278.
17. Put a circle around your answer to this problem.
18. Count out in your normal speaking voice from 1 to 10 backwards.
19. Punch 3 small holes in your paper with your pencil point here   .   .   .
20. If you are the first person to get this far, call out loudly, "I am the leader in following directions."
21. Underline all even numbers on the left side of this page.
22. Now that you have finished reading carefully, do only sentences one and two.

7 Internal Dialogue

Purposes

To engage in internal dialogue in order to:
A. Focus on an attitude, feeling, or area of uncertainty that is a problem for oneself.
B. To gain clarity, objectivity, and, perhaps, a solution to a personal dilemma.

Group Size

Any number can participate in the writing part of this activity. Discussion of the process should be done in groups of ten to twelve persons.

Time Required

One hour total; the first half for writing and the second half for discussion.

Setting

The participants' introspective experience during the writing portion of this activity can be enhanced if they sit with plenty of space between one another. They could be scattered throughout a large room or outdoors on a lawn. The discussion groups that follow can meet wherever convenient.

Materials

I. A copy of Dialogue With Myself for each participant.
II. Several sheets of paper and a pencil for each participant.

Procedure

I. Give a brief introduction concerning "the many selves within us," referring to our occasional need to take time to think through some aspects of ourselves in which we fall short of our own self-expectations.
II. Divide the participants into groups of ten to twelve each.
III. Hand out a copy of Dialogue With Myself and a pencil to each participant. Review the directions for clarity, then disperse the groups, asking them to come together again in thirty minutes for a group discussion.
IV. When the discussion groups come together, a facilitator should be present in each group as discussion leader. The discussion can focus on both the content and the process as follows:
- Assure the participants that sharing the content of their internal dialogues is voluntary and they do not have to say anything.
- Ask if anyone would like to read her or his dialogue to the group so that it can be used as an example for case discussion.

- If a volunteer shares his or her written dialogue (and usually at least one person is willing to do so), then ask the other group members to serve as consultants to the volunteer in seeking further clarification and resolution of the problem.
- Focus on the process of clarification, regardless of content, which occurs as one writes.
- Ask how many members obtained a sense of direction out of their dilemma.
- Compare this process with that of Lewin's Force-Field Analysis (Lewin, 1969; Spier, 1973), which is also used as a means of problem solving and identifying action steps.

References

Lewin, K. Quasi-stationary social equilibria and the problem of permanent changes. In W.G. Bennis, K. D. Benne, & R. Chin (Eds.), *The planning of change.* New York: Holt, Rinehart and Winston, 1969.

Spier, M. S. Kurt Lewin's "force-field analysis." In J. E. Jones & J. W. Pfeiffer (Eds.), *The 1973 annual handbook for group facilitators.* San Diego, CA: University Associates, 1973.

DIALOGUE WITH MYSELF

Instructions: People belong to groups, but in a sense, each of us **is** a group. There are voices within us that clamor to be heard on many of our internal issues — pro and con. By allowing these voices expression, you may be able to select the one which, if listened to, will bring you into the most satisfactory congruence with your central self. This activity will help you to gain objectivity, clarity, and focus on one of your concerns.

Will you please select a topic of great interest and concern to you and tune in to your internal dialogue — the voices that speak pro or con on that issue. Then write the dialogue of the conversation between these internal voices. Now, see whether you can "hear" the two sides of the conversation. Once started, do not hold back but let the conversation flow wherever it may. Some general suggestions that may help you to choose a dialogue topic are:

Why do I treat _____ the way I do, and how can I do better?

Why do I feel the way I do toward _____, and do I have to feel this way?

On the possibility of _____, my optimistic and pessimistic selves say . . .

You do not have to share what you write unless you want to. You can regard this as a private document and write without restraint, but please write in the format of a conversation such as a dialogue from a novel or a play.

8 The Fishbowl

This activity should not come as a surprise to the participants. Include it in the program design and announce it as part of the expected schedule at the first meeting of the laboratory. Because of the presence of observers, the Fishbowl is not just another meeting of the training group (T-group). Instead, it should be regarded as a separate learning device that happens to use T-groups in its format. Secondary gains from this activity are to be found in allaying some of the curiosity about other groups and other trainers, as well as other participants. However, during the period of processing the learnings, such issues should be kept subordinate to the primary purposes of the activity.

Purposes

I. To practice group observation and diagnostic skills.

II. To give and receive intergroup consultation for intensifying the work of a training group.

Group Size

I. This activity uses pairs of T-groups.

II. Three T-groups can use the activity by having two groups observe one group at work in the center and having each group in turn take its place in the center. In this case, the time allotment must be extended by one-half hour.

Time Required

One and one-half hours.

Setting

I. The Fishbowl is most appropriately used after the T-groups have had three or four meetings; in a typical laboratory starting on a Sunday evening or Monday morning, it could occur on Tuesday afternoon. There should be several T-group sessions scheduled to follow the Fishbowl so that the groups can take advantage of the consultation received.

II. In addition to the separate meeting rooms used by the T-groups, a larger room is needed to accommodate the pairs of groups that participate in the Fishbowl.

Materials

I. A copy of the Observer's Guide for each participant.

II. Paper and a pencil for each participant.

Procedure

I. Designate the two groups as Group A and Group B; there should be a facilitator for each group. Ask the members to position themselves in an inner and outer circle, with Group A in the center and Group B on the outside. Distribute paper and pencils to all members.

II. The facilitator for Group B gives each member of Group B a copy of the Observer's Guide.

III. Group A proceeds with its T-group meeting for twenty minutes, and its facilitator participates in his or her usual style.

IV. The facilitator for Group B calls time after twenty minutes and asks the observers to comment. The facilitator for Group A stops the meeting, admonishing the members to keep silent, to listen, to take notes if they wish, and to regard the comments as feedback that may be beneficial. The members of Group B report their observations of Group A. (Time: ten minutes.)

V. The groups and their facilitators reverse positions (Group B moves to the center) and repeat steps I through IV. (Time: thirty minutes.)

VI. After the second round, the two T-groups move immediately to their separate meeting rooms for processing. Points for discussion are:

A. How would you describe the climate of the two groups?
B. What is the basic problem in each group that functions as the group's present, underlying agenda?
C. How can we use the feedback we received to improve our own way of working together?

OBSERVER'S GUIDE

Instructions: Your task is to use your skills as a **group-level** process observer. This means that the comments and behavior of individuals and the content of the meeting become secondary to your main task, which is to critically observe and record **how** the group is functioning and to write **what suggestions** you can make for improvement.

Some group-level processes on which you may get data are (you may note others):

What norms has this group developed for:

   Openness

   Politeness

   Confrontation

How do you see participation?

   Broadly shared

   Paired

   Individualized

How would you describe the group climate?

Does the group show dependence on:
   The trainer?

   Certain members?

Is there counter-dependence (fighting to be free of the power of authority)?

What is the basic, underlying issue in this group?

What are your recommendations for improving the group members' way of working together?

9 Tinkertoys™

Purposes

I. To provide a small-group activity as a nonthreatening task for participants at the beginning of a workshop.

II. To allow participants an expression of their expectations for the workshop.

III. To introduce participants to the practice of processing an activity.

Group Size

Participants work in groups of four to eight each. Any number of groups may be used.

Time Required

One hour.

Setting

Preferably, each group should work at a round table that is large enough to seat four to eight people. If tables are not available, the groups may work seated in circles on the floor. The room should be large enough to maintain separation between groups.

Materials

I. A box of Tinkertoys for each group with the instructions removed.

II. The Process Guide displayed on a flipchart.

Procedure

I. After the groups have been seated, place an unopened box of Tinkertoys on each table.

II. Introduce the activity by saying:

> Work together as a group and use the Tinkertoys to create a symbol of your expectations for this workshop. You have forty minutes to do this, so you may want to begin by discussing what you hope to learn here. Let the symbol that you are creating develop from your discussion.

III. After forty minutes, ask each group to select a member to interpret its symbol to the other groups. As this is done, all participants can move from table to table so that they can see and hear well.

IV. When the groups are reseated, ask them to analyze and discuss the interaction they had during performance of the task. Suggest that they follow the Process Guide (which you have printed on the flipchart) in their analysis.

PROCESS GUIDE

1. What behaviors or statements by others influenced what you thought or did? Be specific and speak to the person who influenced you.

2. What would have helped the group to do better . . .

    during the discussion phase?

    during the construction phase?

Alternatives

I. This activity may be used for other purposes, such as:
   A. Midway in a workshop, ask the participants to make a symbol of their group at its present stage of development.
   B. At the end of a workshop, ask the participants to make a symbol of their chief learnings from the workshop.

10 Marathon

A marathon is a training group (T-group) that meets without a break for six to fifteen hours or more. Emphasis is on continuous T-group activity. The marathon, therefore, is a different and often more intense experience than would be obtained from the same number of T-group hours in a conventional laboratory where the T-group sessions are interspersed with theory sessions, activities, meals, socializing, and rest periods.

Purpose

To provide an intensive T-group experience in a condensed period of time.

Group Size

One T-group, usually of eight to ten people.

Time Required

A designated time of from six to fifteen hours without dispersal of the T-group.

Setting and Materials

The physical setting should be that required by a T-group: quiet, free from distractions, with everyone comfortably seated, and the necessary facilities for refreshments and rest rooms. Coffee, tea, fruit, and sandwiches should be available throughout the marathon.

Procedure

I. Hold the T-group for the designated time without break. The time for adjournment should be known to everyone from the start. Part of the excitement of a marathon is the idea that work will be continuous. Being aware of the time for adjournment will help the group to pace itself through the various phases of a T-group activity.

II. The group and the trainer together can decide whether to take a break for refreshments or to continue working. The same procedure may be followed for bathroom breaks. Collaboratively establishing group norms such as these can become a source of learning for some group members.

III. If breaks of any kind are allowed, impress on the group members that the break is "time for being alone." Pairing during breaks can resolve interpersonal problems and lower the group activity to insignificance.

Alternative Procedures

I. Encourage any participants who wish to fast for periods up to twelve hours or more. This may add clarity or irritability to the thinking and behavior of some members, thereby providing extra dimensions of self-exploration and self-knowledge.

II. Schedule a marathon early in a laboratory as a means of speeding up T-group learnings.
III. Schedule a marathon late in a laboratory when there is a need for more time to deal with group or individual issues, as perceived by the trainer or group members.
IV. Schedule a marathon as an isolated event, such as a group meeting over a weekend. This might extend for as long as thirty-six hours, and members are allowed to take catnaps in the room, with the group's permission.
V. During a marathon, either follow the traditionally unstructured T-group format or introduce games to provide additional personal and interpersonal data.

Evaluation of Procedure

Little evaluation has been made of marathon laboratories in comparison with T-group activities that are spaced through time. The marathon has not yet been subjected to experimental testing on the relative values of massed practice versus spaced practice in this respect. Consequently, trainers are divided on the merits and benefits of marathons.

The marathon should not be regarded as the equivalent of a full human relations training laboratory. It emphasizes only one method of learning — the T-group. Many persons achieve important learnings from the other components of a laboratory, such as the theory sessions, the socializing, and the activities.

11 Structural Interventions

One of the most powerful interventions a facilitator can make is in the physical setting of a group and in the grouping or seating arrangement of the participants. "A change in seating arrangement, for instance, can change the stimulus value of persons, which in turn will modify the inner life of the participants" (Luft, 1966, p. 1). Asking group members to work for a short time in trios can produce a broader pattern of verbal participation and reduce the tendency of some individuals to dominate the interaction. "In one stroke [structural interventions] may change many process elements such as atmosphere, persons confronted, and the group's focus of attention" (p. 1).

A facilitator should use structural interventions regularly with a group but with care based on a prediction of appropriateness and outcome with readiness to face the consequences if the group does not follow such a suggestion. If one's timing and reading of the group are correct, the restructuring will be readily accepted and acted on and the work of the group will have been truly "facilitated."

EXAMPLES OF STRUCTURAL INTERVENTIONS

1. Pairs. Group members are asked to find a partner and then carry out an assigned task together. This often is used during a get-acquainted period or when there is a need to get everyone immediately involved.

2. Trios. When members meet in trios to discuss a topic and then prepare a report on their response or offer questions to the total group, two purposes are served: (1) everyone has a chance to speak; and (2) a degree of anonymity is preserved, since the response or question comes from three persons rather than from an individual. As a consequence, greater depth or intensity is often achieved.

3. Quartettes and quintettes. Dividing a group into subgroups of fours and fives can quickly become useful for obtaining a sense of the meeting or to get a quick reading on attitudes and reactions before coming to a group decision.

4. Sextettes. A group of six is ideal for working on a task. The physical closeness and eye contact aid in communication and the mix of ideas, opinions, and attitudes promotes creative thinking. When one trainer must work for a day or more with a large group of thirty to one hundred persons, an efficient means of obtaining maximum participation and satisfaction is to build teams of sextettes and use them as the basic groups for a variety of learning activities.

5. The silent group. Ask the usually silent members (especially, but not exclusively, in a T-group) to move their chairs to the center of the room and carry on the discussion while the usually vocal ones observe for awhile.

6. Separation by sex. Ask the sexes to separate for a short time and prepare a brief report on their perception of the underlying issues that may be present in the group but are not being discussed.

7. The confrontation pair. Two people may be carrying on a protracted argument, appearing to be far apart in their views. If they are also seated far apart, ask them to move closer together and then to continue their discussion.

8. The new setting. The climate for learning in a training group is determined largely by the psychological relationship, not by the ugliness or the ease of the surroundings. Nevertheless, it is a learning experience for many groups to change the location of their meeting place for one session, and then note whether it makes a difference in the content and feeling of the group activity.

9. Facilitator's position. When a group sits at a round table or in a round circle without a table, it is relatively unimportant where the facilitator sits. However, if the group meets at a long table, it is preferable for the facilitator to sit along one of the long sides, rather than at the head or at the foot of the table, thus avoiding the authoritative connotations of those positions.

If a lecture or general session is held in a long narrow room, then in order to be closer to all participants, the facilitator should be in the middle of the long side rather than at the end of the room.

If all the participants adopt a practice of sitting on the floor, then it is best if the facilitator joins them rather than sitting above them in a chair. At a later time, however, the facilitator may call their attention to the fact that the group can be flexible in this norm as in all others, so that those (including the facilitator) who wish to use chairs will feel free to do so.

10. Other arrangements. The closed circle is usually the formation of choice for free exchange and maximum communication, oral and otherwise. A sense of competition and antagonism is evoked in participants when they are grouped facing one another in parallel lines.

Groups often suggest that they meet outdoors. However, intensive group work is difficult outdoors due to distractions, the difficulty of individuals hearing one another, sunburn, bugs, and excessive relaxation. Such meetings can be tried and then evaluated for their effectiveness.

Reference

Luft, J. Structural intervention. *Human Relations Training News.* 1966, *10*(2), 1.

12 Conference Techniques

Conference planning requires ingenuity and careful design. Variety in format can not only prevent the conference from being repetitiously dull, but it can also improve the effectiveness of communication. The planners of most conferences aspire to more than providing a podium for the speakers; they also want the participants to become involved, to learn, and, ideally, to leave the conference with a commitment to use some of what they have learned.

A collection of designs for varying the structure of conferences is offered here to aid conference-planning committees as they determine their conference objectives and decide how to meet them.

COMPENDIUM OF TECHNIQUES AND SUBTECHNIQUES

TECHNIQUES

The Speech

Definition: A carefully prepared oral presentation of a subject by a qualified person, which, for productive learning, requires careful planning. It is often used with other techniques.

Purposes for which used: (1) present information, identify or clarify problems, and present analysis of controversial issues; (2) stimulate and inspire audience, and encourage further inquiry.

The Forum

Definition: A period of open discussion carried on by members of an entire audience (twenty-five or more) and one or more resource persons, directed by a moderator. It is generally used to follow other techniques (speech, panel, symposium, interview, demonstration, or role play), giving the audience an opportunity to participate. The audience may comment (to be distinguished from a question-answer period, in which the audience is only to ask questions of the resource person), raise issues, and offer information, as well as ask questions.

Purposes for which used: (1) clarify and explore ideas; (2) attain verbal audience participation; (3) have resource persons deal with needs as they arise.

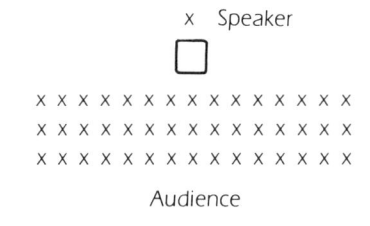

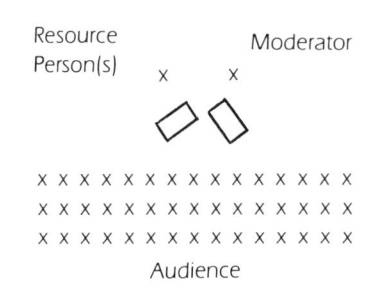

This material has been adapted from **Adult Education Procedures: A Handbook of Tested Patterns for Effective Participation** by Paul Bergevin, Dwight Morris, and R. M. Smith, Copyright © 1963 by Seabury Press. Used with permission.

The Panel

Definition: A group of three to six persons who have special competence in the subject and the ability to express themselves holds a purposeful conversation under the leadership of a moderator in front of an audience.

Purposes for which use: (1) identify, explore, and clarify issues and problems; (2) bring several points of view and a wide range of informed opinion to an audience; (3) gain understanding of the component parts of a topic and identify advantages and disadvantages of a course of action.

The Colloquy

Definition: Two to four resource persons (as in a panel) and some persons from the audience and a moderator. The audience representatives discuss the topics with the resource persons under the guidance of the moderator.

Purposes for which used: (1) stimulate interest; (2) identify, explore, clarify, and solve issues and problems; (3) present to resource people the audience level of understanding topics; (4) have experts deal with needs as they arise.

The Symposium

Definition: A series of related speeches by two to five qualified persons speaking with authority on different phases of the same or related topics. They do **not** speak with each other, but, under the direction of the chairman, they make presentations. A symposium is often used with a panel or forum.

Purposes for which used: (1) present organized information, showing a wide range of authoritative opinion about a topic and setting forth an analysis of several related aspects of a topic; (2) help people to see relationships of aspects of a topic to the topic as a whole; (3) stimulate thinking in persons with similar backgrounds and interests.

Expanding Panel

Definition: A combination presentation and discussion in which six to twelve persons hold a discussion while surrounded on three sides by the audience, followed by an arrangement in which the entire group will discuss the topic. The moderator chooses when to close the panel discussion, then all the participants form into a large group to continue the discussion.

Purposes for which used: (1) identify, explore, and clarify issues groups from twenty to forty in number; (2) secure active participation from a whole audience, especially useful in ongoing class situations; (3) stimulate interest with a situation in which a relatively large group can deal with topics of mutual interest.

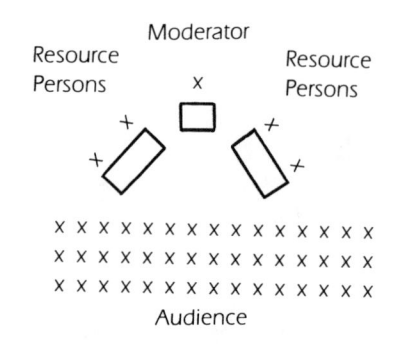

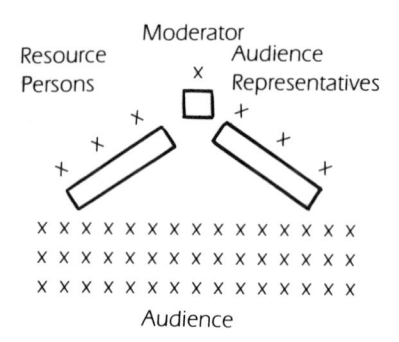

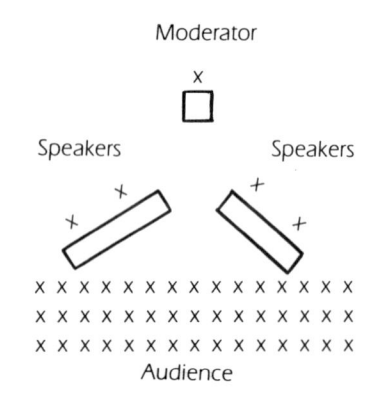

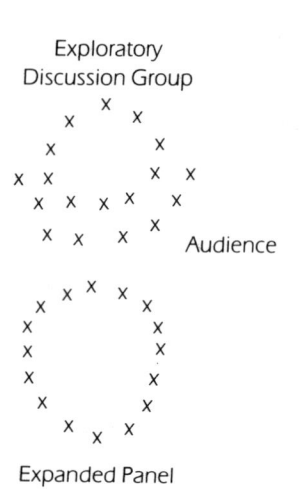

36   *Activities for Trainers: 50 Useful Designs*

Group Discussion

Definition: When engaged in by trained persons under trained leadership, group discussion is a purposeful conversation in which the participants explore, teach, and learn about a topic of mutual interest. Groups usually number from six to twenty.

Purposes for which used: (1) identify, explore, learn about and solve problems and topics of mutual interest in which each participant is both teacher and learner; (2) achieve maximum participation and encourage growth of all participants.

Role Playing

Definition: A spontaneous acting out (without script) of a situation, condition, or circumstance by selected members of a learning group, which emphasizes relationships between people and portrays typical attitudes. Following the role play, the learning group discusses, interprets, and analyzes the action that took place. The emotional impact is greater through role playing than reading or hearing about a situation and sets a frame of mind for self-examination.

Purposes for which used: (1) illustrate interpersonal problems dramatically; (2) gain insight into others' feelings and discover how they might react under certain conditions; (3) develop skill in problem solving and diagnosis; (4) help audience members gain insight into their own behavior and attitudes.

The Interview

Definition: A five-to-thirty-minute presentation for an audience in which an interviewer systematically questions and explores various aspects of a topic with one or two resource persons. The resource persons know in advance the nature of the questions to come.

Purposes for which used: (1) present information informally and provide, through the interviewers, a bridge between the audience and the resource persons; (2) explore and analyze problems, clarify issues, stimulate interest in the topic; (3) gain an authority's impressions of experience he or she and the audience have in common.

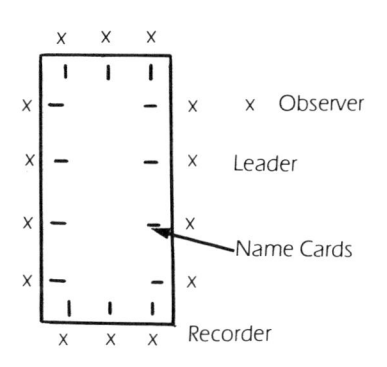

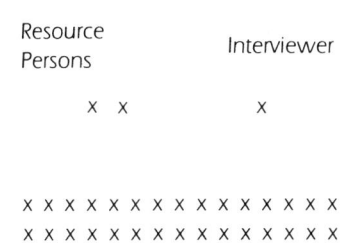

Part 1. Group Dynamics and Laboratory Training

SUBTECHNIQUES

A subtechnique is like a technique, but it is used for a shorter period of time and is used to modify or adapt a technique to the requirements of a particular learning situation. A subtechnique cannot stand alone.

Buzz Session

Definition: An audience divided into small groups (about six members per group) to discuss a topic, or perform a task assigned them (e.g., raise several questions about a speech). They meet briefly, usually not more than ten minutes.

Purposes for which used: (1) gain audience involvement through discussion, identify needs and interest, and receive contributions from those who do not speak in larger groups; (2) enable a large group to evaluate a learning experience.

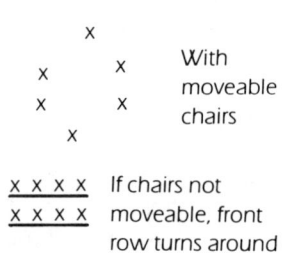

Audience Reaction Team

Definition: Three to five audience representatives who may interrupt the speaker at appropriate times for clarification of obscure points or to help the speaker treat the needs of those present.

Purposes for which used: (1) ensure that an audience understands a subject that might be difficult to communicate or might be presented "over their heads"; (2) interrupt when audience is too large for all to do so; (3) use with speech, symposium, demonstration, or interview.

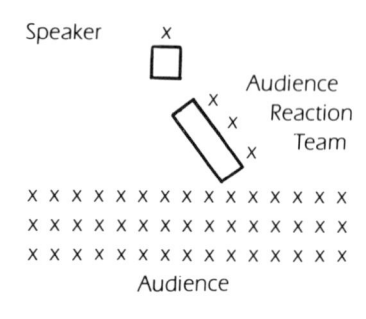

Idea Inventory

Definition: Often called **brainstorming**, this is a spontaneous outpouring of ideas for five to fifteen minutes on a topic of interest or need. As many ideas as possible are recorded but not discussed during this period. Quantity is preferred over quality.

Purposes for which used: (1) to obtain several alternative ideas prior to a decision; (2) obtain many ideas when they are wanted; (3) encourage maximum participation because of nonevaluative character.

Screening Panel

Definition: Three to five persons from the audience discuss the educational needs of the audience in the presence of a speaker or resource person so that the speaker or resource person can adjust the presentation to the audience's needs, interests, and level of understanding or compose the presentation on the spot.

Purposes for which used: (1) use prior to presentations involving the techniques of interview, speech, symposium, or panel and help resource persons or speakers to gain insight into the expressed needs and interests of learning group; (2) involve audience members and encourage them to express their needs.

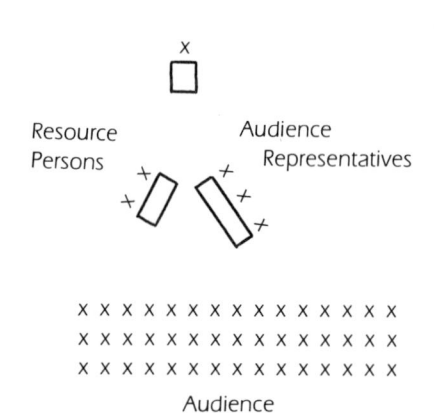

13 Values: Influencing Others

Purposes
I. To identify the limits of an individual's ethical constraints.
II. To compare an individual's ethical value system with those of others.

Group Size
Small groups of six to eight members each.

Time Required
One hour.

Setting
This activity can be used as a staff training session or as part of a series of sessions on value clarification.

Materials
I. A pencil and a copy of Ways to Influence the Thinking of Others for each participant.
II. A blank flipchart and markers.

Procedure
I. Introduce the activity by describing the mental set with which the participants are to approach it:

> You are about to attend a staff meeting and present your case for obtaining a sizeable budget for a project in which you are intensely interested. After your presentation, there will be an open discussion in which you will participate, along with the others. A decision will be reached, and there is a lot riding on it for you. You have a heavy stake in seeing that the decision goes your way.

II. Divide the participants into groups of six to eight persons each. Hand out a copy of Ways to Influence the Thinking of Others and a pencil to each participant. Ask the participants to read the instructions and the list of methods and to ask questions about any item they do not understand.

III. Announce that they have forty-five minutes to complete their lists and discussions.

IV. Use the last ten minutes of the hour for a general sharing discussion and a summary, focusing on the following points:

  A. Read through the list of items and write on a flipchart the items that were marked by only one or two persons.

B. Ask the entire group:
   1. What did you learn about your own ethical boundaries and those of others?
   2. What do you think about trying to obtain laudable ends by using means that others might question?
   3. Have you derived any general principles or a philosophy that can help to guide you in making difficult choices?

WAYS TO INFLUENCE THE THINKING OF OTHERS

Instructions: You are about to attend a staff meeting and present your case for obtaining a sizeable budget for a project in which you are intensely interested. Your presentation will be followed by an open discussion. A decision will be reached and you have a heavy stake in seeing that it goes your way.

Read the following list of ways to influence the thinking of others. Check those items you would be willing to use, either in your presentation or in the discussion that follows.

When all the members of your particular group have completed checking their lists, circle each item that no members of your group checked; these are now eliminated as items that no one accepts. Turn to the column labeled "Group Results" and check all the other items. You can now compare the methods you would use with the methods that at least some of the other members of your group would use. Discuss these and encourage individuals to explain and defend their reasons for using methods you would not use yourself.

I would use this	Method	Group Results
_____	**Honestly express** your aim	_____
_____	**Delay revelation** of your aim	_____
_____	**Conceal** your aim	_____
_____	**Exaggerate** to make your point	_____
_____	**Focus attention** on your issue	_____
_____	**Simplify** by omitting details	_____
_____	Use **symbols** or **analogies**	_____
_____	**Get personal** in your argument	_____
_____	Use **slogans**	_____
_____	Take care with your **timing**	_____
_____	Stage a **dramatic** presentation	_____
_____	Surround yourself with **a cloak of virtue**	_____
_____	**Flatter** those with power	_____
_____	**Ingratiate** yourself to the strong	_____
_____	Present yourself like an **unopposed leader**	_____
_____	**Select** material that supports your point	_____
_____	**Omit** material that weakens your point	_____
_____	**Embellish** your point with flattering examples	_____
_____	**Associate yourself** favorably with success	_____
_____	Use "purr words" known to be liked by your audience	_____
_____	Speak in **glittering generalities**	_____
_____	Appeal to the **self-interest** of authority figures in the group	_____
_____	Raise, and then knock down, easy issues: the **straw man** gambit	_____
_____	Divert trouble by bringing up side issues: the **red herring** principle	_____
_____	**Confuse** others with complexity	_____
_____	**Exclude** those who don't count in the decision	_____
_____	**Distort** the facts when it serves your purpose	_____

I would use this	Method	Group Results
_____	**Illustrate** your points with flair	_____
_____	**Appeal to emotions**, especially when your argument is weak	_____
_____	Be safe by getting **everyone to participate** in the decision	_____
_____	Be **theatrical**	_____
_____	Admit to **no alternatives** to your solution	_____
_____	Create a **band wagon** with known supporters	_____
_____	Play up the **universality** of your approach	_____
_____	Indicate **endorsement** by power figures	_____
_____	**Drop the names** of authorities supporting you	_____
_____	Show that there is **religious sanction** for your idea	_____
_____	Mention that **history proves** you are right	_____
_____	Suggest that **statistics support you**	_____
_____	Stress the **scientific method** in your plan	_____
_____	Think up **proverbs** that support you	_____
_____	State your **facts** in unarguable terms	_____
_____	Promise **written guarantees**	_____
_____	**Vary your approach** according to how the group is responding	_____
_____	Claim that **experience supports** your way	_____
_____	Give a **practical demonstration**	_____
_____	**Threaten** discreetly, if necessary	_____
_____	**Coerce** others with promises or threats	_____
_____	**Command** with eyes, voice, and posture	_____
_____	Appeal that **immediate action** is required	_____
_____	Prepare for a **long seige** of negotiation	_____
_____	Tie your point to a **recent success**	_____
_____	Drive your point in with **repetition**	_____
_____	Knock down opposition with **negative association**	_____
_____	Weaken opposition with **name calling**, either witty or barbed	_____
_____	Silence others with **verbal abuse**	_____
_____	**Insinuate** something negative about opponents	_____
_____	Your point is all good, other points are all bad: the **black-and-white contrast**	_____
_____	**Turn the tables** by showing that arguments against you apply to others also	_____
_____	Use **sneer words** against safe or distant opponents	_____
_____	Imply **guilt by association**	_____
_____	**Ridicule** the arguments or person that opposes you	_____
_____	**Ignore** strong points against you as long as you can	_____
_____	Act like a **martyr** if it looks like you will lose	_____

14 Situational Leadership

Purposes

I. To distinguish between styles of leadership according to situational needs.

II. To discriminate between appropriate leadership style and authentic behavior (that is, just being yourself).

Group Size

From ten to twenty participants or more.

Time Required

One and one-half hours.

Setting

This activity is appropriate for the training of group discussion leaders or as part of a training program in group dynamics.

Materials

I. A copy of the Leadership Style Questionnaire, a copy of Scoring and Analysis, and a pencil for each participant.

II. A blank flipchart and markers.

Procedure

I. Introduce the activity with comments concerning the following issues:

A. In many situations, a group leader is designated, such as a chairperson of a committee, a group discussion leader, or a director of a task force. Should they all behave alike?

B. Some people believe that the best leadership is provided when the leader behaves in an authentic manner. That is, the feelings and behavior of the leader are open and congruent. It is best to be yourself.

C. Others believe that different situations call for different leadership behaviors, even different attitudes, on the part of the leader.

D. We are going to examine this issue, and in the process learn more about the skills of leadership.

II. Divide the participants into groups of five or six members each. A copy of the Leadership Style Questionnaire, a copy of the Scoring and Analysis form, and a pencil are given to each member.

Part 1. Group Dynamics and Laboratory Training

III. Ask one half of the groups to answer the questionnaires from the point of view of a Discussion Group Leader and to write that title at the top of the questionnaire. Ask the other half of the groups to answer the questionnaire from the point of view of a Director of a Task Force and to write that title at the top of the questionnaire.

IV. Announce that they will have forty minutes to answer the questionnaire, score it, and discuss the results in their small groups.

V. You may want to offer assistance to individual members to see that the scoring is properly done.

VI. Reassemble the group for a discussion of the following questions:

A. If any of the members achieved a perfect score, did those individuals feel that some of their answers called for unauthentic behaviors?

B. In what way did members of the group differ in their interpretations or acceptance of the answers?

C. Using group members' contributions, list on a flipchart the goals of a Group Discussion Leader and of a Task Force Director. Then ask the members to determine whether differing behaviors might be necessary to meet these goals.

D. Ask the members to identify some skills that they still need to develop in order to be versatile and professional leaders.

Note: The set of answers in the "Feeling-Oriented" column could be used more fully than they are in this activity, which is directed primarily to basic skills. The Feeling-Oriented answers are generally applicable to the facilitation of T-groups or encounter groups.

LEADERSHIP STYLE QUESTIONNAIRE

You are the leader of a _____

Instructions: There are ten situations described in this questionnaire. Each situation has three alternative actions listed; they are possible attitudes or positions you might have as the group leader or director. Read each of the alternative statements and rank them in the following manner:

Write 3 next to the position you would be **most likely** to take on the statement.

Write 2 next to the position you would be **next most likely** to take on the statement.

Write 1 next to the position you would be **least likely** to take on the statement.

1. The leader of a meeting should:
   - _____ (1) Focus attention on the agenda (either written or hidden).
   - _____ (2) Focus attention on each person's feelings, in order to help the members express their emotional reactions to the issue.
   - _____ (3) Focus attention on the different positions members take and the ways they deal with each other.

2. As a primary aim, the leader should:
   - _____ (4) Establish a group climate in which work and accomplishment can take place.
   - _____ (5) Establish a climate that encourages openness and caring.
   - _____ (6) Help group members to find themselves as members of the group.

3. When strong disagreement occurs between a group leader and a member, the leader should:
   - _____ (7) Listen to the member and try to ascertain whether the task is understood.
   - _____ (8) Try to get other members of the group to express themselves in order to involve them in the issue.
   - _____ (9) Support the person for presenting his or her views.

4. In evaluating a group's performance, the leader should:
   - _____ (10) Involve the whole group in assessing its learnings and satisfaction.
   - _____ (11) Get the group to compare its achievement with the goals it had set.
   - _____ (12) Allow each person to set his or her own goals and performance standards.

5. When two members of the group get into an argument, the leader should:
   - _____ (13) Help them deal with their feelings as a means of resolving the argument.
   - _____ (14) Encourage other members to help resolve it.
   - _____ (15) Allow some time for the expression of both sides, but keep the discussion related to the task and subject matter at hand.

6. The best way to motivate someone who is not performing up to his or her ability is to:
   - _____ (16) Point out the importance of the group's work and your need for everyone's contribution.
   - _____ (17) Inquire into the underlying problem in order to understand the reason for the low performance.
   - _____ (18) Not be concerned; the person will contribute when he or she is ready.

7. A leader's evaluation of a session should focus on:
   _____ (19) The smoothness and efficiency with which the session was conducted.
   _____ (20) Whether everyone contributed his or her ideas and opinions.
   _____ (21) Developing a sense of achievement in both the leader and the members.

8. In dealing with hidden agendas (e.g., minority issues, low motivation), the leader should:
   _____ (22) Deal openly with such issues if they threaten to disturb the relationships in the group.
   _____ (23) Confront the issues quickly so that they do not divert the group.
   _____ (24) Show understanding and get all the members to help deal with the issue.

9. As a goal, the leader should:
   _____ (25) Make sure that all the resources of group members are known and used.
   _____ (26) Draw out controversy and differing opinions that may contribute to the group goal.
   _____ (27) Encourage members to contribute, if they want to do so.

10. The leader's greatest contribution to a group is to:
    _____ (28) Model attitudes and behaviors that shape the group's energy.
    _____ (29) Establish a climate in which true attitudes and feelings are expressed.
    _____ (30) Lead subtly and allow members full opportunity to interact.

SCORING AND ANALYSIS

Instructions: In the columns below, next to the number of the situation, enter the number of your ranking for each action statement. Please note that the order of the numbers in the columns does not correspond with that of the questionnaire itself. In question 3, for example, the column positions are, from left to right, (7) - (9) - (8), not (7) - (8) - (9).

Situation	Action Statement	Rank	Action Statement	Rank	Action Statement	Rank
1.	(1)	_____	(2)	_____	(3)	_____
2.	(4)	_____	(5)	_____	(6)	_____
3.	(7)	_____	(9)	_____	(8)	_____
4.	(11)	_____	(12)	_____	(10)	_____
5.	(15)	_____	(13)	_____	(14)	_____
6.	(16)	_____	(17)	_____	(18)	_____
7.	(19)	_____	(21)	_____	(20)	_____
8.	(23)	_____	(24)	_____	(22)	_____
9.	(25)	_____	(27)	_____	(26)	_____
10.	(28)	_____	(29)	_____	(30)	_____
Total		_____		_____		_____
		Task Force		Feeling Oriented		Discussion Group

GROUP LEADERSHIP STYLE

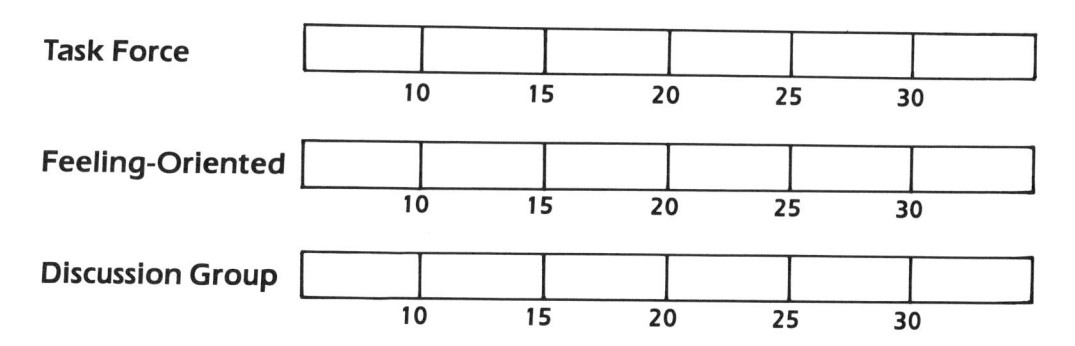

Task Force
10   15   20   25   30

Feeling-Oriented
10   15   20   25   30

Discussion Group
10   15   20   25   30

Transfer your total score for each of the columns to the bar graphs by shading the bar to the point representing your score. For comparison purposes, if you have a score of less than 30 in the type of group leadership that was assigned to you, then either your intuitive choice was erroneous for that situation, or you may have a real and logical difference of opinion with the "book answer." The real question is: Can you change your leadership style according to the needs of the situation?

15 Checking Out Nonverbal Communication

In a human relations training program, nonverbal activities are often used to heighten awareness, but they are seldom focused on for the purpose of enhancing the communication process. This activity establishes a group norm that, over successive meetings of a training group, permits a fuller exploration of the meanings and significance of nonverbal behavior than is usually the case.

Although the use of clues from nonverbal behavior can be very effective for judging unexpressed feelings, attitudes, and relationships, research suggests that *one's interpretation of the clues can be wrong* a good share of the time. By establishing a norm by which one's interpretation can be checked out, a member is enabled to learn to interpret nonverbal communication with appropriate caution.

Purposes

I. To become aware of the constant flow of nonverbal communication in a group.
II. To assess the relative degree of one's accuracy in interpreting nonverbal communication.

Group Size

From seven to fourteen persons.

Time Required

This procedure can be repeated occasionally during successive meetings of a training group (T-group).

Materials

A card labeled Nonverbal Inquiry for each member and for the trainer.

Procedure

I. At an early meeting of a T-group you are training, find an opportunity to intervene with a brief input on the interpretation of nonverbal behavior, making the following points:
   A. People are drawing conclusions from nonverbal behavior all the time. Sometimes they are accurate, sometimes not.
   B. To illustrate, what are your conclusions about some of the nonverbal behavior going on in this room right now?
      1. Get some reports and some interpretations from members of the group.
      2. Check them out for accuracy.

II. Hand each member a card labeled Nonverbal Inquiry and instruct the group as follows:
   A. These cards may be used whenever a member wants to check out his or her interpretation of the meaning of another's nonverbal communication at that moment. The card permits and legitimizes an interruption of whatever else is going on at that time. Just hold it up, and we will let you talk to whomever you wish about the nonverbal communication you are receiving.
   B. To check out a nonverbal communication, one says to another, "I notice that you are . . . (specify the nonverbal *behavior*)." "Does this mean . . . (specify your interpretation)?"
   Note: The give-and-take exploration may take some time. Some people may see this as an interruption of the T-group work; others may see it as an important aspect of T-group work.
III. Ask the group members whether they will agree to use this procedure for a specified period of time in each meeting, e.g., the first fifteen or the last fifteen minutes. The group can determine the time at the beginning of each session.
IV. With the group's consent, institute the procedure. It will probably be used for several sessions, after which a renegotiation of the agreement may be necessary. Usually the new agreement will dispense with the cards, and the checking-out procedure will become a part of the natural flow of the communication in the group. If so, then the establishment of a new norm has been accomplished.

16 Dream Collection

Purposes

I. To use the dream life of participants as data for learning.

II. To use the dreams as validating data for the laboratory experience as a whole.

Group Size

A discussion is conducted for all participants in a general session toward the end of the training laboratory.

Time Required

One hour.

Materials

Written reports of dreams collected from volunteers each day of the training program.

Procedure

I. On the first day of a training program you are conducting, ask for volunteers to participate in the following experiment with dreams:

The experiment will consist of volunteers writing down whatever they remember of their dreams each morning and depositing the report in a collection box. Their anonymity will be protected by the use of code names instead of real names on their written reports. Selections from the dreams submitted will be used for a learning event toward the end of the training laboratory.

Note: If the training staff agrees to participate, this can be mentioned too and may encourage others to join in the experiment.

II. To those who volunteer, give the following instructions:

Select a code name to put on your dream report each day. Use the same name throughout the experiment. On each report, write the code name and the date it is submitted. The date will indicate that the dream occurred during the night just passed. Write down as much of the dream as you remember, even if it is a fragment. Do not add anything in order for the dream to "make sense" or to give it continuity. Write *no dream*, if you cannot recall any. It is best to write your report immediately on awakening, before you do anything else. Remember that we may use your dream for discussion, so avoid writing your own name on the report.

III. Place a collection box at the entrance to the breakfast room or in the location where the dream reports can best be collected each day.

50   Activities for Trainers: 50 Useful Designs

IV. Collect the dreams each day and file them in chronological sequence. If cooperation falls off, you may have to make a subsequent announcement to remind the volunteers.
V. Schedule an hour in general session for analysis and discussion, preferably on the day before the end of the training program.
VI. Be prepared to read aloud in sequence several selections from the dream collection. Participants usually enjoy this sharing, especially if they know that it has the consent and approval of those who were part of the experiment. Note the following points:

- Earlier dreams are shorter and fragmentary, although later dreams may be quite long.
- Symbolism in early dreams may be very obtuse and uninterpretable, although later symbols may be easily perceived.
- Sexuality becomes more overt in later dreams.
- The trainer becomes more overt in later dreams, as may some of the participants.
- Signs of anxiety may decrease through the sequence, and evidence of joy and pleasure increase.

VII. In leading the group's discussion of the dreams, focus on the following points for learning:

A. Do these dream sequences suggest that the participants in the experiment were becoming more open as the lab went on?
B. Were there signs of reduced anxiety and, therefore, a reduction in defenses?
C. Is more openness and a reduction in anxiety congruent with lab goals?
D. What significance can be made of the appearance of the trainer in dreams?
E. Is there evidence of increased self-acceptance?

17 A Nature Walk

Purposes

I. To provide group members with an intense experience of sensory awareness.

II. To become more appreciative of beauty in the commonplace of nature.

Group Size

Not more than twelve and probably not fewer than six participants.

Time Required

One hour. This activity can be offered in the late afternoon as a free-time event.

Setting

Outdoors, preferably in an area containing woods, a stream, boulders, an old road, etc. The facilitator should scout the territory carefully beforehand (see Procedure).

Procedure

I. This activity should be conducted with a volunteer group. It can be offered through an announcement or a bulletin-board notice and described as "an unusual nature walk." It is assumed that trust in you has been developed by the group and that curiosity will entice persons to attend. People often come with placid expectations of a bird-watching tour, or expect to have trees and wildflowers identified for them. Answer any questions beforehand by simply saying that it will be "unusual."

II. When the group has gathered, give the following instructions:

> This will be a nonverbal experience. You may communicate with one another by touch or gesture, and I encourage you to share whatever you find important, but do it without talking. During our walk, try to use all your senses more than you usually do: smell, touch, listen, and even taste. Look for things you usually overlook and immerse yourself in whatever is at hand. Let us go in single file to start, and I will lead the way. Follow my clues and pass them back along the line.

III. Lead the way around a route previously scouted. If the terrain is sufficiently varied, it might include the following elements, but with ingenuity, you might find many others.

- Entering dark woods.
- Smelling moss, mold, and the underside of a bark on a fallen log.
- Lying on the ground, looking at the sky through the trees.
- Listening to discriminate the sound of running water from the sound of wind in the trees.
- Gathering around a rain puddle in a rutty road; using it as a mirror; watching spiders and other life forms in the water.

- Walking through shrubs or high grass and coming out into the open.
- Sitting down to contemplate a colorful mushroom or lichen.
- Tasting a dandelion leaf, a pine needle, and straw.
- Gathering in a quiet glade for a group hug.
- Sitting quietly so that each person can become intimately acquainted with the square foot of ground in front of him- or herself.
- Returning to "civilization."

IV. This activity provides many participants with an emotionally laden peak experience. It is, therefore, best to dismiss the group without comment. Some participants may want to sit quietly and savor the experience for fifteen or twenty minutes. During the next few days, be ready to listen to any reflections that the participants may have.

18 A Nonverbal "Who-Am-I?" Experience

Purposes

I. To use fantasy under conditions of partial sensory deprivation as a means of examining one's self-concept.

II. To share the experience in order to achieve understanding and acceptance of it.

Group Size

This activity is useful after several group meetings, when the members have developed some degree of trust. It is suitable for a T-group of ten to twelve persons or for a general session of twenty to thirty persons.

Time Required

Thirty minutes.

Setting

A large carpeted room where people can sit comfortably on the floor, separated from each other to some degree.

Procedure

I. Introduce the activity with comments similar to the following:

   A. A self-concept is a complex mixture of impressions and conclusions that each of us has developed about herself or himself, almost without realizing it. Some of these ideas are readily available to us, while others are barely known to us. However, these self-concepts influence our behavioral choices all the time as we attempt to maintain consistency within ourselves. In this group, we will take some time to explore the question of *Who Am I?* more fully than is usually possible in the rush of everyday events.

   B. In order for us to turn inward for this self-examination, we will try, as much as possible, to exclude external stimulation and get away from the daily events that intrude on us. To do this, we will use a little of the technique called sensory deprivation.

II. Ask the participants to sit comfortably on the floor, with legs crossed and elbows on their knees. In this position they can use their fingers to close their ears. Give the following instructions:

   Make sure you are seated comfortably. After I have given you these directions, I want you to close your eyes and press your fingers tightly over your ears. When you have done that, listen to the sounds of your body. You may hear your breathing or your heartbeat, and you may see things on the inner surface of your eyelids. After listening for a while, slowly begin to consider the question, *Who Am I?* Allow your mind to toy with this idea freely; do not force your thought or try to think about it. Just let happen whatever happens. I will clap my hands after about three minutes to let you know the time is up. Then we can talk about the experience. Start now.

III. After three minutes, clap your hands and stop the action.

IV. If the group is small, encourage each person to tell of the experience. If the group is large, divide the participants into groups of three each and ask them to share and understand the experience.

Note: Typically, the reports indicate the individual's increased awareness of isolation, loneliness, and separation, of individuality and aliveness, and of mortality. The fantasies frequently take the form of symbolic imagery rather than words, and sometimes they are a projection of a central problem the individual is working on.

19 Whole-Brain Function

Through the media of popular literature, the findings of research on brain function are becoming common knowledge. It is presently believed that the brain is divided into two hemispheres, the left hemisphere (LH) and the right hemisphere (RH), and that each half specializes in different types of thinking. The individual's typical educational and developmental experiences encourage the use of the LH, which emphasizes a logical, orderly approach to the world and its problems. The RH is usually left to its own devices, since its intuitive, nonrational leaps have not been found to be of predictable use and control in the marketplace. We are learning that a combination of the two approaches can have practical consequences in creativity, an enrichment of daily living, and more effective problem solving.

The exercises offered here are designed to encourage the kind of preferences and learning activities usually attributed to RH functioning. No claim is made, of course, that these exercises actually stimulate the right brain to action. Without the use of biofeedback or other brain-monitoring equipment, there probably is no way to know if there is any brain activity at all. We must believe, like Descartes, that "I think, therefore I am!" There is common agreement, however, that the two hemispheres perform different learning activities, which are listed at the end of this chapter in Differences in Brain-Hemisphere Learning.

Research with encephalography suggests that RH activity increases under conditions of assuming a quiet, relaxed state, closing one's eyes, and imagining a calm scene. It is recommended, therefore, that before any of these exercises are undertaken, the facilitator take five minutes or so for the group to achieve such a state of readiness.

Purposes

I. To identify the differences between left-hemisphere (LH) and right-hemisphere (RH) brain function.

II. To practice and develop a more frequent use of RH function.

III. To apply RH function to problem solving.

Group Size

Most of these exercises can be performed by an individual, but better learning is achieved by doing them in a small group of six to eight persons.

Time Required

The exercises are not intended to be done all at once. Each takes from twenty to thirty minutes, including discussion and reflection. They may be done sequentially, as in a class, or in meetings over a period of time.

Materials

Materials are described in the procedure for each exercise and they include:

III-B. A bag or dish of popcorn for the group, a slice of apple or a cup of coffee for each participant;

VI. Paper and a pencil for each participant;

VII. Marking pens and art paper for each participant. (Fingerpaint can be used, but it requires water and rags.)

VIII. A clear glass, three-quarters full of water.

Procedure

Direct the following exercises, one by one, telling the participants to do each of them slowly. Pause for discussion after each exercise. Instructions for the facilitator are shown in italics. The other statements are directed to the participants.

I. Tell yourself to salivate (LH). Then, imagine eating a juicy slice of lemon (RH).

II. Use the brainstorming technique and imagine as many uses as you can for the following:

A brick;

A plastic one-gallon milk jug;

A string of questions asked by a child (for example, when a child asks "Why is the sky blue?" and responds to each of your subsequent answers with "Why?", how many answers can you give?).

III. Get reacquainted with your body:
   A. Take off one shoe and sock. Note the sensations in your body as you sit that way for a while. Walk across the room. Dance.
   B. *Pass around a bag or dish of popcorn and ask the participants to:*
   Eat some with your left hand (or with your right hand if you are usually left-handed);
   Pay attention to the spatial relationships that you notice between bag, hand, and mouth.
   Repeat the exercise with slices of apple or cups of coffee.
   C. Comb your hair in a direction that is opposite to your custom.
   D. Think of other means of doing something physical in a different way than usual. Note the reawakening of sensations of touch, temperature, movement or strain in your muscles and joints, etc.

IV. The next time you feel an itch, instead of scratching it, notice the total body reaction that you experience in its presence. What does it tell you about *interconnectedness*? Note also how often you scratch an itch *before* you can remember to do this. What does this indicate about the body's self-caring mechanisms?

V. *Play a group game: choose an object, such as a shoe, and have each participant complete the sentence, "Life is like a shoe because . . ." Repeat with other objects, then complete the game by using the name of a person in the group: "Life is like Diane because. . ."*

VI. *Distribute paper and pencils and ask the participants to:*
Write a paragraph that describes something, such as a scene or an event. Use no punctuation, pay no attention to sentence structure, and omit logical development, such as time sequence and cause-effect. Then read the paragraph and see if the impact — the essence — comes through.

VII. *Provide large sheets of paper and marking pens to each participant.* Create a picture in the direct, intuitive style of Zen. Sit and look at the paper until the essence or insight of the thought or emotion you want to portray enters your consciousness. Then, in a few large strokes and without hesitation, transmit that essence to the paper.

VIII. *Place a clear glass that is three-quarters full of water in the center of the group.* Look through the sides of the glass and tell what you see. Do not give associations or interpretations; just describe what you *see.* Try to rid yourself of any preconception of what you should be seeing and describe exactly the image that is there.

IX. *A group has a problem and you want them to see it in a new light as a possible aid to finding a resolution.*
Sit quietly and visualize the problem as a formless shape in the center of the group.
  A. Describe how it looks or feels to you.
  B. If it had a handle, what would it be like?
  C. Does the handle present a clue to resolution of the problem?

X. Mass-produced art, literature, television, and advertising use standard methods for creating new combinations out of familiar elements. We can take a more flexible approach to our problems by using some of these methods. Sit quietly and think of a problem you have been concerned about. Then ask yourself:

What would it be like if I . . .

reversed it	rearranged it
turned it upside down	stretched it
flattened or rolled it	took it apart
chopped or powdered it	turned it around
connected some of its parts	used the opposite
did it backward	omitted most of it
felt differently about it	combined it with . . .

DIFFERENCES IN BRAIN-HEMISPHERE LEARNING

LEFT HEMISPHERE **RIGHT HEMISPHERE**

Learning Activities

intellectual	emotional
rational	nonrational (fantasy, curiosity)
logical	intuitive
linear	nonlinear
sequential	diffused
discriminative	integrative
temporal	timeless
verbal (using words, sentences)	imaginative (images)
deductive	inductive (experiential)
explicit	tacit
active	receptive
analytical	synthesizing
digital	analogous
goal-centered	experience-centered

Learning Preferences

defining	seeing metaphors
clarifying, separating	unifying (Gestalt)
organizing	combining in unusual ways
questioning	wondering
verifying	creating
planning	dreaming
writing	drawing
talking	singing

Data from pages 6 and 7 in MINDWAYS: A GUIDE FOR EXPLORING YOUR MIND by Louis M. Savary and Margaret Ehlen-Miller. Copyright © 1979 by Louis M. Savary and Margaret Ehlen-Miller. Reprinted by permission of Harper & Row, Publishers, Inc.

20 Practice in Saying "No"

Purposes

I. To develop skill in saying "no" to requests.

II. To acquire a range of options on how to say "no."

III. To gain experience in saying "no," so that such behavior will be more available in the future.

Group Size

This activity is done in pairs of groups. Learnings are rich if the participants can be placed in groups of six each.

Time Required

One hour.

Setting

A large room where groups of six participants can talk without one group disturbing another.

Materials

I. A pad of paper and a pencil for each participant.

II. A blank flipchart and markers for each group and for the facilitator.

Procedure

I. Ask participants to sit in circles of six persons.

II. Indicate which groups will be paired together. If there is an odd number of groups, distribute the members of one group among the other groups. Having five or seven persons in a group is all right.

III. Introduce the exercise with the following comments (and then reveal the goals of the exercise):

> People often feel pressured and complain about their lack of time to get everything done. Often, they blame this on their not being able to say "no" to requests from others, which increases the demands on their time. In this session we are going to learn how to say no without losing friends or feeling guilty.

IV. Instruct the participants to do the following (and write an example on your flipchart):

A. On a sheet of paper, write *From:* and your name. Then write *To:* and the name of a person in the other group. Prepare a similar request form addressed to each person in the other group.

B. Now your task is to write a request to each member of the other group. You can discuss your requests among yourselves, or you can keep some requests private. You have six minutes for the task. Be both realistic and original in your requests. Here are some examples:
1. I would like to talk with you about a problem I have at work that I think you can help me with.
2. I would like to play tennis with you during our free time this afternoon.
3. Will you go for a walk with me tonight after the evening session?

V. When the requests have been written, instruct the participants as follows:

In a moment I am going to ask you to stand up and mingle with the other group. Engage each member in a brief conversation, expressing your request, and then hand the written request to the person for future reference. As people make requests of you, do not accept any of them at this time. Respond with some delaying comment, such as "That might be interesting" or "I will have to let you know." You have fifteen minutes to complete all your conversations.

VI. After fifteen minutes, tell the participants to return to their own groups. Provide each of the groups with a marker and flipchart paper and assign the following task:

Discuss among yourselves different ways to say "no" and make a list of them. There are ways that are blunt, or soft, or a postponement, and ways that show consideration or do not. Some ways give hope, while some give none. Write actual words and phrases that might be used.

VII. After six or eight minutes, give the following instructions:

A. Now, individually plan how you will say "no" to each of the requests you received. Write notes on the request forms, so that you will not forget, and vary the methods you choose to use. The ground rule is that you must say "no" to each of the requests.
B. When you are ready, mingle, engage in a brief conversation as before, and say "no" according to your commitment. You have fifteen minutes to complete your conversations.

VIII. Ask the paired groups to meet together to discuss the following aspects of the experience:

A. From the point of view of the receiver, what types of "no" responses were the easiest for you to accept?
B. From the point of view of the one saying "no," which ways worked the best for you?

IX. Allow about ten minutes for the group to process the experience and then ask for some reports for general sharing. Also ask for comments on how this experience has helped the participants in preparing to say "no" on future occasions.

21 The Relationship Contraption

Purposes
I. To experience building *open* and *closed* relationships.
II. To learn behaviors that contribute to each kind of relationship.

Group Size
Participants work in groups of three each (trios). Any number can participate, even a large group in an auditorium.

Time Required
One hour.

Setting
This theory presentation and demonstration can stand alone as a lecture-demonstration on interpersonal relationships, or it can be introduced early in a training laboratory to enhance the work of T-groups.

Materials
I. A flipchart and markers for the facilitator. The Relationship Contraption Chart may be displayed on an overhead projector or, for a small group, it may be prepared on a flipchart before the meeting.
II. Paper and a pencil for each participant.

Procedure
I. Prepare the room ahead of time, arranging the chairs in groups of three.
II. Introduce the activity by briefly presenting a theory that encompasses the following ideas:
   A. An interpersonal relationship is like a *contraption* that two persons construct together.
   B. The contraption relationship, or relationship contraption, exists in and of itself, outside the persons and their personal attributes.
   C. The relationship contraption is dynamic in the sense that it has moving parts and can be changed by tinkering.
   D. Both parties in a contraption share ownership, and every relationship is unique to the persons involved.

62   *Activities for Trainers: 50 Useful Designs*

III. Display The Relationship Contraption Chart and make the following points:
   A. All relationships can be considered as being located along a continuum that ranges from open to closed.
   B. Ask participants to call out words and phrases that characterize the ends of the continuum (and list them on a separate sheet of flipchart paper), such as:

   For *open*: free, direct, varied, expressive . . .
   For *closed*: tentative, routine, tight, superficial . . .

   C. Using the left-hand column of The Relationship Contraption Chart, point out that the degree of openness depends on the answers to four questions:
      1. Who is concerned about the topic of the conversation?
      2. What is the time perspective?
      3. How do we use our feelings?
      4. How personal will we be?
   D. Clarify other parts of the chart and answer questions until you are sure that it is understood.
IV. Give a copy of the Relationship Contraption Task Sheet to each trio and read the instructions aloud before each task is begun.
V. Allow ten minutes for the trios to engage in their conversations. Call for a time-out at five minutes, and at eight minutes.
VI. Have all the participants join together for a general discussion of the experience, and ask them the following questions:
   A. Were you able to alter the relationship according to The Relationship Contraption Chart? How did you do it?
   B. Did all three members react similarly to alterations?
   C. In other groups, and especially in T-groups, can you recall how attention and involvement varied in accordance with the Relationship Contraption Chart?
   D. How can this knowledge be of use for diagnosis or remedial intervention in groups when you are a group leader or participant?

RELATIONSHIP CONTRAPTION TASK SHEET

Work on the following tasks in your trios, with two people holding a conversation and the third serving as an observer. The roles may be shifted from task to task.

A. **Task I.** Conduct a three-minute conversation at the **closed** end of the scale. The observer is to note any verbal or nonverbal behaviors that are not at the closed end of the scale and report these to the other two members. During the reporting period, the two conversationalists talk about how they felt while working in a closed manner. Three minutes are allowed for the reporting and the discussion.

B. **Task II.** Conduct a conversation at the **open** end of the scale. As before, continue this for three minutes and then use another three minutes for the observer's report on the conversationalists' violations and feelings and for their responses and discussion.

C. **Trio Reports on Tasks I and II.** How can you describe your reactions and feelings in the two different modes, closed and open?

D. **Task III.** All three members in your trio are to converse on a topic of their choice, paying attention to the dimensions of **topic, time frame, feelings,** and **personalizing**. Intentionally alter one or more of these dimensions, without announcing that you are doing so, to see if the sense of relationship also alters. You will have ten minutes for this and the facilitator will give a signal from time to time of "one-minute time-out!" to allow you to check with one another to see if you are feeling similarly along the closed-open continuum.

THE RELATIONSHIP CONTRAPTION CHART

Making and Breaking Emotional Contact

Certain kinds of interaction lead to an experience of close emotional contact while other kinds do not. This chart outlines some of the marks of interactions that make or break emotional contact. Think of each scale as a continuous one with the amount of emotional contact increasing toward the right end. Each scale modifies the others. The amount of emotional contact, thus, does not vary with any single scale but depends on the interaction of all scales.

Amount of emotional contact depends on →

	NO EMOTIONAL CONTACT ←———— SUPERFICIAL ————→ CLOSE EMOTIONAL CONTACT
1. TOPIC: nature of	Generalizations: concepts, ideas, intellectualization / External, public information: objects, events, behavior / Inner, private information: perceptions, feelings, thoughts
stakes	Low risk: unimportant topic / Moderate risk: mildly important topic / High risk: crucial topic
experience	Something neither has experienced first-hand / Something one of us has experienced first-hand / Something both of us have experienced first-hand / Directly concerns you **or** me / Directly concerns you **and** me — our relationship
2. TIME FOCUS OF CONVERSATION	No time perspective, as in generalizations, jokes / About the distant past or future / About the near past or future / Openly describes what we are doing, thinking, or feeling in the immediate present
	Has no relation to what is now happening between us / Increases our awareness and understanding of what you and I are doing and feeling right now
3. COMMUNICATION OF FEELINGS: in words	No attempt: we ignore, avoid, and deny feelings / Indirect, disguised: via playing, teasing, quipping, needling, joking, pretending, and use of sarcasm / We openly describe our feelings and try to understand the other's feelings
in actions	No attempt to communicate feelings by actions / Frequently communicate feelings by actions
congruence	What the person says and does, and his or her involuntary emotional expressions are not congruent; they send different, even contradictory, messages / What the person says, does, and his or her involuntary emotional expressions are congruent; all indicate the same emotional message

---

The Relationship Contraption was conceived in 1965 by John L. Wallen.

Part two
The Training of Trainers

22 A Guide for Designing a Training Program

When a training staff works together to design a program, it must achieve a high level of efficiency and creativity. Trainers typically are interested in doing something new, rather than repeating a tried-and-true procedure. They search for variations in methods used in the past, or they fashion an entirely new approach to a training topic. Such staff interaction provides some of the greatest rewards in training because the members can learn from one another and enjoy working with a congenial and professional group.

Unfortunately, the amount of time allotted for design purposes is often short, and much has to be done in the time available. A much-needed tool is a guide for staff members that not only describes what should be done but also suggests the sequence to be followed. Such a guide is provided here. It can be used in the training of new trainers, and experienced trainers may find that they follow this procedure automatically. For them, a quick review of the guide will help ensure that essential steps are not overlooked.

DESIGNING A TRAINING PROGRAM

If the staff members for a training program are new to one another, initial time (perhaps as much as an afternoon or an evening) should be scheduled for them to do their own team building.

The staff typically must take up the following considerations, in approximately the order given, as it prepares a training event.

1. Assess needs.
2. Set training goals.
3. Assess staff resources and skills.
4. Select training strategies and place them in the order they will occur in the program (prioritize).
5. State the objectives for each module of the program.
6. Predict the time schedule for each element of the modules.
7. Allocate a staff member who will be responsible for each element.
8. Assess the logistical elements.
9. Define primary client concerns.
10. Provide for evaluation.

Schedule time for future planning and checking sessions of the staff. Few programs run their course without alteration. When will the staff get together? Can it be done during working hours so that meetings will not consume all available free time or go on late at night?

1. Assess needs
    - What data do you have on the participants' jobs, back-home environment, age, sex, race, religion?
    - What are the participants' expectations for the training program?
    - Has a precourse questionnaire been administered? Have you seen the program announcement?
    - What further information do you need to obtain at the beginning of the program?
    - What can you anticipate from the participants in the way of mood, volunteerism, readiness?

2. Set training goals
    - Discuss and write a set of goals for the program, usually not more than five, and have them ready for use in the first session.
    - Agree among yourselves on the difference between goals and objectives.
    - Be explicit about values, the methods to be used, and any ground rules.
    - Establish trainer responsibilities as seen by the trainer.

3. Assess staff resources and skills
    - What training aids and devices have staff members brought with them?
    - What special skills and interests exist among staff members?
    - If certain unusual modules are needed, who can handle them?
    - Make a list of what resources are needed and the resources that are available to see if there are any gaps.

4. Select training strategies and prioritize them
    - This is the heart of the design: what should come first, second, etc.
    - Block out the time schedule on newsprint and start filling it in.
    - Begin with known elements: meals, free time, and perhaps time for back-home planning and evaluation.
    - As other elements are filled in, look at the schedule's balance, flow, and required energy level.
    - Mornings are better for theory; afternoons for activity; evenings for nonverbal events and T-groups.
    - If T-groups are included, theory sessions should be selected to enhance the T-group activity in its predictable phases.
    - One thing should lead to another. Will the experience of the participants be one of growth and development, or will it seem to them that they are getting a series of unconnected inputs?

5. State the objectives for each module
    - This may be done by the staff, through discussion, or by the staff member responsible for a specific module.
    - Ideally, the objectives should be specific and measurable: "By the end of this period you should be able to . . ."
    - Present the objectives to participants at the start of each session. Knowing where they are going will help them to learn better.

6. Predict the time schedule for each element
    - This should be specific: introduction, ten minutes; forming groups and giving instructions, five minutes; working on the task, forty minutes; etc.
    - On a larger scale, review the schedule to see that sufficient time is available for what is planned, for each element.
    - Provide for "fillers." Is more time available than the work will consume? Avoid planning so much that the participants feel hurried.

7. Allocate staff responsibility
    - Generally, all staff members participate in the first session, and all should be visible. Planning the opening session often takes a large portion of the total planning time.
    - For subsequent modules, individual staff members or pairs can volunteer to take responsibility.
    - All staff need not participate in planning every session.
    - Often a staff member will want to try to conduct a type of session for the first time as a means of learning or stretching.
    - No one should be overburdened or under utilized. This is a good time to establish a norm regarding when and how staff members can help one another. When a staff member is up front, presenting, is it OK for others to interrupt?

8. Assess the logistics
    - Space: large rooms, small rooms, comfort, convenience.
    - Materials: handouts, pencils, newsprint, nametags, workbooks, masking tape, flipcharts on easels, magic markers, tape recorder and tapes, reference materials.
    - Housekeeping details: breaks, meals, physician, sleeping comfort, etc.
    - Administration: registration, money, travel, personal supplies.
    - Recreation: bar provision, indoor-outdoor resources, alone time, and socialization.

9. Define primary client concerns
    - Who is the primary client? Who is paying for this?
    - What is this client's expectations? How will you communicate?
    - Does your design to this point meet these expectations?
    - What contact will you have with the client before, during, and after the program?
    - Will the client be expected to take action as a result of the program?
    - Are you and the client clear on your contract?

10. Provide for evaluation
    - Will you evaluate as part of the design:
        By obtaining postmeeting reaction sheets for each module?
        By obtaining a daily rating of satisfaction or learnings?
        By obtaining an end-of-program evaluation?
    - Each of these needs preparation. Who is going to do it?
    - Any provision for follow-up?
    - Is there a requirement for a report to the primary client?
    - Do you anticipate that the design as planned will meet the goals stated?

23 A Memory Bank for Facilitators

Over a period of time, a facilitator's skills may become rusty. A useful intervention is forgotten, or well-practiced types of interventions become so overused that they become stereotyped. Experienced process consultants, group-discussion leaders, and T-group trainers often think back over a group session that has just ended and wish that they had remembered to do one thing or another which, at the time, slipped their minds. They could have used a list of trainer interventions. Such a list is offered here as a memory-jogger to rebuild one's mental set and behavioral repertoire from time to time.[1] This list of trainer interventions can be used as a device for renewing your potential as a facilitator for responding appropriately, especially when you feel the need to get back into the role of trainer after a lapse of time. Many of the items reflect a theoretical base with which other trainers might disagree; therefore it is not intended as a cookbook recipe to be followed exactly. Instead, if you read the list through prior to beginning work with a new group, it can serve to renew your conceptual framework and increase the professionalism of your interventions.

TRAINER INTERVENTIONS

1. Go with the energy flow.
2. Never use "us" or "we" statements as a trainer.
3. An intervention that couples you to a participant invites focus on you as the trainer and is usually to be avoided.
4. A trainer briefly taking a participant role is only effective when the group has coalesced. You can make a participant statement, but should remain in the role of the trainer.
5. An intervention listing a number of feeling words helps people who are having difficulty identifying feelings.
6. When a difficult issue surfaces, an individual-oriented intervention is preferred to one at the group level. Such issues are hard for a group to deal with.
7. When someone fails to absorb feedback, one type of intervention that is useful is: "Did you hear . . ." or "What did you hear?"
8. An interruption or sudden shift of topic might call for: "Could we give people a chance to pick up on . . ."
9. When a participant makes a trainer intervention, such as commenting on the group process, you can:
   A. Intervene to get at the participant's feelings.
   B. Ask for an explicit hypothesis.

---

[1]The list is an adaptation of one compiled and recorded by participants in a 1976 NTL Institute Training Theory and Practice Laboratory in Bethel, Maine. Florence Hoylman and Howard Lamb were the trainers.

Note: In a mature group, participant interventions are more likely and in later stages of a group need not be as heavily discouraged as earlier in a group's life.

10. Directly answering the questions of a participant can lead to an intellectual discussion. At that point, asking the group for feedback may be a way out.
11. If two issues are being developed simultaneously, indicate this to the group and ask for priority.
12. If participants jump over someone's issue or fail to follow through, a "Hey, you just switched the topic!" type of intervention may be useful.
13. It is usually preferable to start a session with a no-focus type of statement (if an opening is used at all).
14. When a there-and-then type of statement leads to an argument with the trainer, an intervention that focuses on the personal dynamic ("What is going on between us?") or a group-level intervention ("Do you all want to stay with this?") will be helpful.
15. Occasionally, breaking into a seminar type of group discussion can be useful, if the group is well formed and if it is made explicit that you are doing so for a short time.
16. If, as trainer, you set some norms at the outset, then your interventions should model those norms.
17. If one participant is receiving feedback and another starts to work on him too, offer space, i.e., "Do you want to hear from other people?" and then come back.
18. Co-trainer statements should not directly follow one another.
19. The trainer should pick up on things to go back to.
20. When, as trainer, you become lost, state how you feel about it.
21. If a member is briefly absent, use the time to let others get in touch with themselves: "Time for contemplation."
22. When a reluctant participant joins in, use a "Glad to have you . . ." type of intervention (but without using those words).
23. Summary type interventions can be useful to provide clarity, check out accuracy, and stimulate learning.
24. You can demonstrate anger to set the norm that expression of anger is OK in the group.
25. Some participants react better to restatement and clarification interventions than to the usual behavior-feeling response. Adjust interventions to fit the person, including your language.
26. If a participant contribution seems inappropriate, i.e., leads away from the energy source, you can provide space by checking it out: "Do you want to get into that now?"
27. As the trainer, you can make use of a range of nonverbal responses.
28. When a group is working with a reluctant participant, the tendency is to be overly civilized, although the underlying feeling is hostility. You can bring out the underlying hostility or at least remove the polite facade.
29. The trainer should avoid accepting participant labels or analogies.
30. A trainer's response can be human; you should not attempt to be an objective, unfeeling robot. (How can the trainer be anything but human?)
31. When an "I like you" type of statement is made, it may be necessary to pull out more data and a wider range of support. Such a statement may act to cloud the issue.
32. There frequently will be defenders for a reluctant participant, and you may have to keep them from directing energy away from that participant.
33. When a participant states that he or she wants to be off the hook, it is not an automatic signal that you should go that way. You will need more data than that. An opportune intervention is: "Maybe you can move on from here."

34. When a participant says, "Others in this group," follow up on what is meant by "others."
35. Be alert to nonverbals, and also do not limit your focus to one thing or one person. A trainer should develop the habit of surveying the entire group periodically (every three minutes, for instance).
36. If a there-and-then statement goes by, the trainer may choose to legitimize and redirect it: "I think it was important for you to cover that, but I would like to come back to..."
37. Starting a meeting with a relaxation type of activity can backfire by getting people so relaxed that they have difficulty getting into anything. A better approach is to have them look at each other and attempt to be in contact with issues. Relaxation also tends to focus on positive feeling while avoiding the negative.
38. If a trainer states that an issue is difficult, then it becomes more difficult for the group to deal with the issue.
39. When a sensitive issue arises, some participants may try to leave it by bringing up another issue. At this point, it may be best to use an intervention that either gives permission to explore the issue or holds off new issues: "We have several things we need to get into..."
40. As the trainer, avoid doing things that invite focus on yourself.
41. There is no simple way to arrive at a T-group consensus decision, so avoid interventions that require a group answer.
42. When you are stuck on your own feeling, share it and indicate a desire to go on.
43. Avoid the use of lab jargon with a confused participant.
44. When an intervention does not get any response, try rewording it.
45. When a participant has picked up a nonverbal communication and wants to work on it, the participant's consciousness can be raised by forcing her or him to be more explicit about the behavior-feeling.
46. An "I don't trust the group" statement suggests a trust or self-trust issue in the speaker that can be picked up on at some point.
47. A high energy person who directs communication toward a reluctant participant can produce even more blockage. This may require a restatement or redirecting type of intervention.
48. A group-level intervention must be descriptive rather than interpretive. A trainer can describe group behavior, but should avoid placing an interpretation on group behavior.
49. Group-level interventions require a lot of management or follow-up.
50. Dialogue between judgmental and nonjudgmental persons may lead to issues over labels. This communication problem may be overcome by a restatement type of intervention.
51. People who are unaware of their feelings need an accurate picture of their verbal and nonverbal behavior. Give lots of feedback. Ask them to describe their physical feelings: "Can you tell me what is happening within you as you hear what we say to you?"
52. When the group is well formed, you can impose yourself on the group in the form of a short lecturette.
53. Reluctant members' behavior tends to arouse the concern of others, including the trainer. Do not concentrate so heavily on a reluctant member that you overlook others.
54. Group-level process conceptualizations can be useful as interventions.

55. You can encourage a participant with "I see you as learning from this," particularly if the participant is trying to direct attention away.
56. For a response of "I can't talk about personal problems," a possible intervention is: "Right, concentrate on the process. The idea is to become aware of feelings. Let's talk about them."
57. Where two people are in an issue, but are unable to communicate, it may be necessary to bring others in to work on it.
58. Toward the end of a lab, it may be best to focus on those who have not had as much discussion time. An intervention with an active person might be, "You have shown competence in handling that and others might need the time more."
59. "Why" statements invite intellectualizations (head trips).
60. When you are in a period of high energy, stay with your left-brain functions: be logical, objective. During low energy periods, you can make more use of the right brain: be intuitive and flow.
61. Do not develop fixed notions of where the next session will go. The trainer should neither set a group agenda nor force an issue that he or she insists must be present.
62. Do not accept participants' involvement in paired intimacy. There are a number of alternatives:
    A. Have them verbalize what is happening.
    B. Get into the issue they are experiencing.
    C. Put them into a figurative bubble and go on to the group.
63. A trainer does not have to remain in the same physical location. A move can be a very effective intervention.
64. A report from an earlier event in the group's history, such as last night at dinner, tends to have been so worked out beforehand that it is not likely to be useful.
65. An "I'm afraid of hurting x" remark may call for an "If you really care..." type of intervention.
66. Toward the end of a lab, if a person finally wants to work with the group on something after not having participated earlier, it may be best to suggest "taking it home." Continued group support will reduce the intensity of feeling. However, leaving the feeling or issue unworked will increase the likelihood of recall and possible resolution later.
67. For every situation there is a range of alternative interventions open to the trainer; interventions should not be viewed in either-or terms.
68. You cannot learn a list of useful interventions to be used under specific circumstances because interventions are highly situational. Trainers should strive first for authenticity for themselves and then for professionalism in diagnosing the situation and selecting an appropriate intervention.
69. A failure to intervene is not going to destroy the learning experience. Trust the process. Err on the side of too few rather than too many interventions.
70. A good stance for a trainer is to look only occasionally at the person speaking and to spend most of the time looking at the rest of the group.

24 Sample Guides for Group Observation and Evaluation

A skilled group member is one who is able to combine the functions of participant and observer. As a participant, the individual contributes to the group process through verbal and nonverbal interaction. As an observer, the individual notes the emerging process, diagnoses individual and group needs, and meets those needs through further participant contributions. Simultaneously, the member strives to meet his or her own needs in the group interaction. It is apparent that during a group meeting, a skilled group member is a very busy person who is drawing on a great number of skills.

Programs of training in human interaction and group dynamics often focus more on participant skills than observational skills. However, observational skills form the basis for group diagnosis and deserve the attention of trainers. Observational skills also serve to assist in processing, that important period in an experiential learning program when action is halted in order to examine *how* the people worked together and to extract cognitive learnings from the experience.

A written guide is a helpful device to employ either when participants are asked to serve as observers or during a process period. Such a guide helps to focus attention on significant features of the experience. It can include space for taking notes; and it can be put into a notebook and taken home. A guide can help to start discussion, but it need not limit the bounds of discussion. It suggests, but it does not restrict. It also provides an important avenue for learning and retention for those whose cognitive awareness is best triggered by visual and written cues, in contrast to those who may learn adequately from aural and affective cues such as those provided by the activity itself.

Unfortunately, the preparation of guides is often regarded as a chore by trainers, with the result that the guides are given only hurried attention. There are few standard, all-purpose guides. The central learning feature(s) of each activity must be lifted out by the trainers for processing, or the critical incident(s) or basic group issue must be identified for its own unique analysis. Therefore, the sample guides given in the following pages are not offered as panaceas but as stimulants for the trainer who wonders, "What shall I ask the participants to look at?"

Each guide is preceded by a short explanation of where and how it could be used. In the event that they fit your particular need, the guides are presented in a form ready for duplication. If they cannot be used as presented, it is hoped that the content and format of the guides will stir your creative juices to produce the best guide to bring out the best learnings in your participants. Sample guides are included for the following purposes:

    A. Group observation: external observers.
    B. Group observation: participant-observers.
    C. Group observation: group growth.
    D. Process guide: organization diagnosis.
    E. Action research guide: improving a series of meetings.
    F. Workshop evaluation: standard type.
    G. Workshop evaluation: special type.

A. GROUP OBSERVATION: EXTERNAL OBSERVERS

The term external observers refers to persons who sit outside a group for the purpose of observing interaction. They do not participate in the interaction until called on to make a report to the group. External observers may be members of the group who are only temporarily acting as observers, or they may be total outsiders such as a T-group that observes another T-group (see activity 8, "The Fishbowl").

Guides 1 and 2 are particularly useful in a T-group fishbowl activity, although they could be used with any other type of group, if it is interested in the dimensions of its interaction that are examined by these guides. Guide 3 is useful either in a fishbowl activity or within a T-group itself, with one member serving as the observer.

As a minimum goal in a training program oriented toward group dynamics, all participants should probably be expected to develop skills in observation as indicated in these three guides.

GUIDE 1
GROUP OBSERVATION: EXTERNAL OBSERVERS

Participation. Look for differences among members in the amount of their verbal participation.

Who are the high participators?

Who are the low participators?

Indicate those who seem to shift.

Influence. Influence and participation are not the same. Some people may talk a lot yet not be listened to by others; some may speak only a little, yet others tend to listen to them.

Who are the high-influence members?

Who are the low-influence members?

Atmosphere

How do you characterize the group atmosphere? (Examples: warm, hostile, dependent, confronting, accepting, low-energy, etc.)

What behaviors do you note that support your characterization?

If something were needed to change the atmosphere, what would it be?

GUIDE 2
GROUP OBSERVATION: EXTERNAL OBSERVERS

Subgroups. Look for patterns in which certain individuals tend to consistently agree or disagree with certain other members.

Who tend to agree with and support one another, forming a subgroup?

Who tend to disagree with and oppose one another?

Insiders and Outsiders

Who are the people who seem the most "in?" Why do you think so?

Who are the people who seem the most "out?" Why do you think so?

Are those who are "out" influencing the group in any way?

Basic Issue.

Often there is a basic, underlying issue on which the group is working, such as dependency or counterdependency toward the trainer, or finding status within the group, or testing the members' emotional depths and establishing norms. What do you think the basic issue is for this group in its present stage of development?

GUIDE 3
GROUP OBSERVATION: EXTERNAL OBSERVERS

1. How are feelings handled in this group?

    Expressed? If so, how?

    Suppressed? If so, what is the evidence?

    Ignored? Did you notice feelings that were not picked up by the members?

2. What does the nonverbal behavior suggest to you?

    What nonverbal behaviors did you notice? (Examples: gestures, posture, eye direction, etc.)

    When did verbal and nonverbal behavior not coincide?

    Did members occasionally respond to a nonverbal message?

3. Who influenced the group?

    By initiating the topic or direction for the group:
    By attracting the group's focus:
    By helping in some way (gatekeeping, clarifying, standard setting):
    What was the influence of the quiet members?

B. GROUP OBSERVATION: PARTICIPANT OBSERVERS

Guide 4 provides direct feedback to named members of a group and is, therefore, most appropriate for a T-group. A member of the group is asked to serve as an observer. This person sits outside the group, avoids participation for a short period (about twenty minutes), and then presents an observer's report.

This guide probably covers too many dimensions for observation to be done by one person. It is better to use one observer for items 1 and 2; then, at a later time, have another person use items 3 and 4 and a final observer use items 5 and 6. As a result, more people have an opportunity to serve as observer. The group also receives unexpected feedback, since the members do not know ahead of time what features will come under scrutiny.

GUIDE 4
GROUP OBSERVATION: PARTICIPANT-OBSERVERS

1. Rank the three individuals who have contributed the most to this meeting.

    1.
    2.
    3.

2. Rank the three individuals who have contributed the least.

    1.
    2.
    3.

3. Rank the three individuals who seem to have the most awareness of their own feelings and the effect of their behavior on others.

    1.
    2.
    3.

4. Rank the three individuals who seem to be the least aware of their own feelings and the effect of their behavior on others.

    1.
    2.
    3.

5. Rank the three individuals who are most influential.

    1.
    2.
    3.

6. Rank the three individuals who are least influential.

    1.
    2.
    3.

C. GROUP OBSERVATION: GROUP GROWTH

Guide 5 is an instrument designed to be filled out by all members of a T-group rather than by a single observer as done with the previous guides. Copies of Guide 5 may be completed by group members at the conclusion of every other meeting. (Members might become disenchanted with it if it were used too frequently, such as after every meeting.) At the middle and at the end of the training program, the results may be summarized (averaged) and shared with the group members. Typically, the ratings move from the left to the right of the scales as the group matures.

Guide 5 has also been used to bring out the disaffected member(s) in a group. If some person's ratings are consistently lower than those of most of the other members, it is an indication that something is wrong. There probably will be behavioral symptoms as well, but to approach some people directly would only evoke a set of defenses such as denial. However, with the ratings as objective data, one can approach the issue as a problem for the group, and there is likelihood of dealing constructively with the issue and with the person's problem.

GUIDE 5. A GROUP-DEVELOPMENT SCALE
GROUP OBSERVATION: GROUP GROWTH

Instructions: Each of the following scales represents a continuum of behavioral criteria used to measure the growth of a group. Rate the stage of growth of your group by circling the number on each scale that you believe describes the attitudes and behavior of most group members.

Distrust	1 2 3 4 5 6 7	Trust
Not Free to Talk Openly	1 2 3 4 5 6 7	Free to Talk Openly
Apathetic & Disinterested	1 2 3 4 5 6 7	Actively Interested & Concerned
Competitive	1 2 3 4 5 6 7	Cooperative
Want to be Directed or Resent Being Directed	1 2 3 4 5 6 7	Members Feel Responsible & Contribute What They Can

84   Activities for Trainers: 50 Useful Designs

D. PROCESS GUIDE: AN ORGANIZATION DIAGNOSIS

In supervisory or management training, the design often includes an activity that requires the participants to organize themselves in order to perform a task. (The "House of Cards," activity 39 in this series, is one example. Other well-known examples that are not included here are the "Tower Building" and some versions of the "Tough Battler.") A great amount of interpersonal and organizational data is generated in these activities, but the process period is often limited to an examination of only the interpersonal, with little attention given to organizational dimensions.

Guide 6 focuses on organizational data. It introduces the participants to organizational level concerns, to the concept of organizational issues that are shared by many, and to the differing perceptions that members of an organization may have about structure.

Materials: A blank flipchart and markers; a sheet of paper and pencil for each participant.

GUIDE 6: EXAMINING YOUR ORGANIZATION
PROCESS GUIDE: ORGANIZATION DIAGNOSIS

Instructions: One way to process the organizational experience you have just had is to perform an organization diagnosis and find out what was functional and what was dysfunctional about the organization you created.

1. Individually, write answers to the following questions on a sheet of paper, but do not sign your name.

    A. What did you **like** about your organization? List two or three things.

    B. What did you **not like** about your organization? Again, list two or three things.

2. Collect all the answers and have someone read them aloud while another person lists the "likes" and "dislikes" on a flipchart.
3. Look for items on the lists that are mentioned by several people. These represent the real strengths and weaknesses of the organization.
4. What could you have done to have avoided the issues on the "dislike" list? Discuss each of these items in turn.

5. The following issues frequently occur on the agendas of organizational team-building sessions. Are they also on your list?
    - Leadership and power.
    - The division of labor and overlapping of job responsibilities.
    - The decision-making process.
    - How feelings are handled.
6. Can you draw an organization chart that everyone agrees to?

E. ACTION-RESEARCH GUIDE: IMPROVING A SERIES OF MEETINGS

This guide may be used after every session of a group that is meeting in a sequence of meetings, such as a T-group, a task force, a committee, a staff meeting, or a class. When Guide 7 is used as an action-research instrument, the facilitator ensures that the forms are completed at the end of each meeting, but no signatures are asked for. The facilitator summarizes the results and feeds the summary back to the group at the start of the next meeting. The group may choose to benefit by the recommendations that are made, thus trying to improve the quality of their meetings. If they are successful, the average of the rating scales will move from left to right.

GUIDE 7. MEETING REACTION SHEET
ACTION RESEARCH GUIDE: IMPROVING A SERIES OF MEETINGS

Instructions: This is an action-research method of improving our discussion sessions. Think back over the session and indicate the degree of your satisfaction with it by marking the scale. Reflect your feeling level as accurately as you can by circling a number on the seven-point scale of satisfaction.

```
         1        2        3        4        5        6        7
Not                              Moderately                        Very
satisfactory                     satisfying                        satisfactory
at all
```

What should the group do to improve the next session?

The results of this survey will be provided to the group at the beginning of the next session.

F. WORKSHOP EVALUATION: STANDARD TYPE

The four questions in Guide 8 are the essential minimum for any lab or workshop evaluation. The guide asks participants for information about their likes, dislikes, recommended changes, and the utility of their learnings. Most evaluation forms are much more complex, but the data from this form will be of use both to trainers and to the client. In spite of its apparent simplicity, participants who take it seriously do not find it an easy form to complete. Therefore, the trainer who uses it should offer it with appropriate gravity and indicate that the information obtained will be read and used in the planning of future programs.

GUIDE 8. EVALUATION FORM
WORKSHOP EVALUATION: STANDARD TYPE

Instructions: Indicate your evaluation of this lab or workshop by writing your responses to the following statements:

1. What I liked about the lab:

2. What I did not like about the lab:

3. What I would change about the lab:

4. How I plan to use what I have learned in this lab:

G. WORKSHOP EVALUATION: SPECIAL TYPE

This evaluation form is constructed on the hypothesis that after a busy week or so in a training program, participants may not readily remember the topics or content that were covered, but they can recall the feelings they experienced. They may also be able to associate feelings with the events that aroused them. For this reason, Guide 9 is made up of sentences to be completed by describing events that triggered various emotional reactions. About half of the sentences ask for emotions that are positive, half require negative emotions. Some could be either, i.e., anxiety may be regarded by some trainers as motivating toward learning, or it may be regarded as debilitating.

A disadvantage of Guide 9 is the considerable time it takes to summarize the results. However, trainers who have used it say that the quality of the information is superior to that collected by other evaluation forms they have used, and they have been able to redesign a workshop easily on the basis of these results.

GUIDE 9: FINAL EVALUATION
WORKSHOP EVALUATION: SPECIAL TYPE

Instructions: Recall the events of the program and what you were feeling at the time and complete the following sentences:

1. During this program I felt most involved (forgot about myself) when:

2. I felt most anxious when:

3. I felt most afraid when:

4. I felt happy when:

5. I felt most left out when:

6. I felt sad when:

7. I felt disgusted when:

8. I felt surprised when:

9. I felt irritated when:

10. I felt successful when:

11. I was bored when:

12. I was curious when:

25 Training Group Discussion Leaders

For many of today's conferences, a consultant is called in to facilitate the conference as a whole. Some types of conferences rely heavily on small group discussions but lack trained discussion leaders. In this case, the consultant is asked to spend a few hours training a selected group of people in the skills of leading a group discussion. There may also be a need for the group discussion leaders to arrange for group observers and a group recorder.

Persons new to the role of discussion leader usually ask the same questions: "What do I do if the group members don't talk?", "What do I do with someone who talks too much?", and "How will I keep them on the topic?" However, the discussion leaders may forget to ask "How should we start?" and "How should we stop?" The following design for training discussion leaders is aimed at giving them a grasp of their role and function.

Purposes

I. To present an outline of the functions of a discussion leader.
II. To provide materials for study and reflection.
III. To participate in brief preview experiences for skill training.

Group Size

Ten to fifteen participants.

Setting

Chairs arranged in a circle for all participants.

Materials

I. A blank flipchart and markers.
II. A pencil and a copy of Suggestions to the Discussion Leader for each trainee.
III. A copy of The Group Observer for each trainee (optional).
IV. A copy of The Discussion Recorder for each trainee (optional).
V. A name tag or card for each participant.

Time Required

Two hours.

Procedure

I. You (the facilitator or consultant) open the training session by presenting on the flipchart the following Basic Conditions for a Group Discussion.

　A. A clear topic of interest to the group.
　B. Group members who differ in their opinions.

94　*Activities for Trainers: 50 Useful Designs*

- C. A climate of acceptance to promote freedom of expression.
- D. A discussion leader who gets things started and then serves primarily as a guide.

II. Lead the participants sequentially through the following list of the discussion leader's functions, encouraging questions and comments as the ideas are developed.

The discussion leader's functions are to help the group get started, to help establish a climate of work, and to keep the group on the track so that its objectives are achieved.

1. Establishing a climate.
    a. Check the room for comfort, ventilation, lighting, and seating.
    b. Arrange seating in a circle, if possible, so that people can see one another's faces.
    c. Ask the members to write their names on name tags or large cards and to wear or display the tags.
    d. Ask the members to give brief self-introductions and produce interest in this activity by asking probing questions of a few.
2. Clarifying the topic for discussion.
    a. If the group has a single topic, write it on a flipchart.
    b. If there are several things to do, write the agenda where all can see it.
    c. Check to see that the topic or agenda is clear to all.
3. Making a few comments to set standards, such as the following:
    a. It will be helpful if we all feel free to give our opinions.
    b. Let us view differences of opinion as valuable.
    c. Besides talking, we can listen and learn from one another and try to build on the ideas of others to advance our thinking.
    d. (If the group is expected to make a report, present this as a goal but emphasize that the discussion is equally important to any product such as a report.)
4. Getting started.
    a. A way to start is to rephrase the topic in the form of a question and say, "Now let's start by hearing from someone on . . .?"
    b. At this point, the discussion leader should remain silent and let the group members take responsibility — and someone will, unless the discussion leader gets in the way by filling in the silence.

III. Allow the trainees to discuss the suggested ideas to their satisfaction or until they start to branch out into other specifics. At that time, hand out Suggestions to the Discussion Leader and a pencil to each trainee.

- A. Go through these suggestions one by one, elaborating ad lib for clarity and understanding.
- B. Set up a brief role play for one or two of the suggestions. Suggestions that lend themselves to this treatment are item 2: the overly long talker, and item 9: encouraging individual ownership of opinions by making "I" statements. Ask four members to form a sample group and coach one of them to be the problem member. Choose a fifth person to act as the discussion leader who intervenes. After the intervention, the group discusses the best way to handle the situation.

IV. If the discussion group is expected to make a report, hand out The Discussion Recorder to each member. Ask the discussion leaders to assign the role to members of their groups. The Discussion Recorder form is fairly self-explanatory but should be reviewed in detail with the discussion-leader trainees so that they can answer questions and brief the recorder for the group.

V. Will the discussion group use a process observer? This is doubtful, but you may wish to hand out The Group Observer and review it with the discussion-leader trainees for the additional learnings it contains for them.

VI. End with a brief summary emphasizing the following:

A. The discussion leader should stay in role and not become a participant.

B. The discussion leader should guide unobtrusively and not become a focus for the group in place of the topic.

SUGGESTIONS TO THE DISCUSSION LEADER

1. Your job is to encourage interaction among the group members, not interaction with you; therefore:
   - When someone is speaking, look at the other members of the group, rather than at the speaker.
   - Do not make a reply to each comment by a group member. Wait for someone else to do so. If necessary, ask the group, "Any reaction to that?"
2. If someone talks overly long, interrupt by saying, "I'm losing the point you are trying to make. Can you state it in twenty words or less?"
3. Encourage interaction by moving away from center stage. After identifying the topic, throw out a general question and then sit down or move to the back of the room.
4. If someone disrupts with too much humor, jokes, and wisecracks, enjoy it for a while and then say, "Now let's get down to business."
5. When questions are asked directly of you, refer them back to the group; say, "Someone here must have a response to that."
6. Use a flipchart or blackboard as a "group memory." As points are well taken, or agreed on, jot them down in a list. This gives the group a sense of progress.
7. If you think you have grasped a complex point someone has tried to express, clarify it for the group by saying, "Let's see, if I understand you, you are saying . . ."
8. Avoid making personal comments that may be taken as disapproval, condescension, sarcasm, personal cross-examination, or self-approval.
9. Insist that people take personal ownership of opinions. Train the group members to say, "I think . . .," not "We think. . ."
10. Watch for platitudes or generalizations that sound good but do not further an understanding of the topic. They show a lack of discriminating thought. Ask, "Can you go further into that?" or "What do you mean?"
11. If there is a debate about the meaning of words, probe for the feelings behind them.
12. Summarize periodically, or ask someone else to do so. Sometimes this can be done by asking, "Where are we at this point?"
13. Do not allow an inference or conjecture to pass as a fact. Always look for the hidden assumption in another's statement and ask about it.
14. Do not insist on having the last word.
15. Do not show approval or disapproval of someone's contribution. You are not there to reward or punish.

THE DISCUSSION RECORDER

The **recorder** makes a written account of the **content** of discussion — the subjects discussed and what the group says about them. The recorder is concerned mainly with the ideas that emerge as discussion develops. Secretaries usually note only points of decision and topics that are discussed; recorders do more. They note the significant comments that are made concerning each topic. The report at the end of a session is usually given as a summary.

Clues for Recorders:

1. Report the essence of **what was said about** each topic. Do not try to report **every** point. Jot down the ones that were important in developing the topic and those on which there was agreement or conflict. This calls for selection and organization.
2. It is not necessary to record **who** said something.
3. Record points on which opinions differed.
4. Record points of agreement and decision.
5. Record points on which the recorder is not sure of group opinions.
6. Be ready to report at any time **during** the discussion and at its conclusion. Feel free to raise questions during the report, such as "Is this the point you were making?"

This material has been adapted from **Adult Education Procedures: A Handbook of Tested Patterns for Effective Participation** by Paul Bergevin, Dwight Morris, and R. M. Smith, Copyright © 1963 by Seabury Press. Used with permission.

THE GROUP OBSERVER

The **observer** makes a written account of what happens as participants explore a subject. Observers fix attention on one specific aspect of the activity — **how we carry on.** They observe the process of teamwork and do not interrupt the meeting unless called on by the group to review a situation that develops as the team pursues its task. They are usually asked to report their observations at the end of the session for purposes of evaluation. Participants can then discuss obstacles to their learning and teamwork.

Clues for Observers:

1. Watch for forces that seem to help or hinder productive teamwork and learning. A simple check list of situations and teamwork behaviors is helpful, such as the following:
   - Is the atmosphere tense or relaxed? Why?
   - Is participation fairly balanced? If not, why?
   - Do we look at each other? The leader? The floor?
   - Do we help each other express ourselves?
   - Do we stick to the point?
   - Are we listening actively?
   - Do we depend too much on the leader?
   - Do we both ask and tell?
   - Who is being left out?
   - How does the leader affect the group?
   - How does the group affect the leader?
   - Are purpose and goals clear?
   - Does the outline help or hinder?

2. The observer's report raises questions about what happened so **the group** can discuss why and what to do next time. Be impartial. Do not state what should have been done. This is for the participants to determine.

3. Some references to the content of the discussion may be unavoidable, but do not keep a running record of things said.

4. Use neutral and impersonal references to describe what has happened. (Only if freedom and acceptance have truly developed can names be used.)

5. Sit where you can observe participants' faces.

6. Give examples of **good** teamwork as well as poor.

This material has been adapted from **Adult Education Procedures: A Handbook of Tested Patterns for Effective Participation** by Paul Bergevin, Dwight Morris, and R. M. Smith, Copyright © 1963 by Seabury Press. Used with permission.

Part three
Cross-Cultural Training

26 A Cross-Cultural Experience

Purposes

I. To establish an intentional culture and, while doing so, to become acquainted with the norms, the standards, and the concept of culture universals.

II. To experience an intercultural event.

III. To generalize understandings about cultural interaction to intercultural experiences of the present and the future.

Group Size

A minimum of twenty persons; the maximum number for ease in management is about forty.

Time Required

Six hours. A meal is part of the activity.

Setting

Separate rooms for the Pink and Green Groups to use during the planning period. A large room for the Embassy Reception.

Materials

I. Blank name tags in two colors: pink for one half of the group and green for the other half.

II. A copy of the following handouts for each participant:
Form Your Own Culture (either Pink Group or Green Group)
Cultural Universals
Concepts Shaping the American Way of Life

III. Paper and a pencil for each participant.

IV. A glass of wine or punch for each participant.

Time Schedule

I. Planning period (groups in separate rooms): Two hours.

II. Embassy Reception (groups meet together): 45 minutes.

III. Lunch or dinner (members stay in role).

IV. Individual group processing in separate rooms: One hour.

V. General session for processing (groups not in role): Two hours.

Part 3. Cross-Cultural Training 103

Procedure

I. Before the start of the activity, prepare a registration list, assigning participants to the Pink or Green group. Persons from the same organization should be separated, and there should be a balance of age, sex, and race in each group.

II. As participants arrive at the registration desk, give each one the following items:
   A. A name tag in the appropriate color for the group assignment.
   B. A copy of Form Your Own Culture to match the assigned color.
   C. A copy of Cultural Universals.

   Note: Take care that members of the two groups do not see one another's instruction sheet for Form Your Own Culture.

III. Direct the participants to their respective rooms for planning.

IV. Allow the groups two hours for planning. Facilitators may observe each group but should avoid influencing either group.

V. Announce the opening of the Embassy Reception and invite the groups to attend.

VI. Allow the reception to run with as little intervention as possible. The facilitators act as preoccupied hosts. You may welcome the participants at the door, serve them wine or punch, and suggest that they mingle and get acquainted, but you do little else.

VII. After forty-five minutes, announce the end of the reception and ask the participants to go to the meal (regularly scheduled at this time) and to stay in role during mealtime.

VIII. Participants return to the large room to receive instructions for processing. Give paper and pencil to each person. Facilitators should have ready a large copy (use flipchart paper) of the following instructions to give to each group after the instructions have been read to the group as a whole:

   Processing Guide

   1. Talk about your experience and your feelings as you got acquainted with the other group.
   2. List the characteristics of the culture of the other group. Bring this to the general session in one hour.
   3. What difficulties did you have in staying in your own cultural role?

IX. After one hour of separate group processing (facilitators may sit in to observe during that time), call the two groups together for a general session. Begin by having the members of each group share their lists of the other group's characteristics.

X. Process the learning to raise the following points:
   A. What cultural features of each group worked to help or to hinder the following:
      - Communication
      - Friendship
      - Flirtation
      - Respect
      - Trust or mistrust
      - Potential for developing a working relationship.
   B. What are some of the real cultural influences on yourself which may have interfered with your ability to assume the characteristics of an artificial culture?

XI. Hand out Concepts Shaping the American Way of Life to aid in the discussion of real cultural influences.

XII. Generalize to intercultural experience of the present and future, e.g., black-white, Latino-American, or American-foreign.

FORM YOUR OWN CULTURE

Pink Group

Your group task for the next hour or so is to **form your own culture**. The task for the other group during this time is the same. At the end of this planning period, you are invited to an Embassy Reception where your group and the other can meet together and get acquainted.

A culture is the totality of the norms, standards, and behaviors that operate in a society. These attributes distinguish a society's members, individually and collectively, from other societies and cultures. The Cultural Universals handout will assist you to develop your own distinct culture. You will heighten your uniqueness as a culture if you maintain the following ground rules:

1. When you are interacting with a member of your own group, be as open, spontaneous, and helpful as you can. Both give and seek support from your group members, whether you are alone with them or in the presence of outsiders.

2. When interacting with members of the other group, do everything you can to improve your understanding of them by being friendly and receptive. Openness in oneself invites openness in others, so strive for a free and outgong society in this workshop.

3. Be supportive of one another in this effort. Inquire, express curiosity, and offer more of your private world than is your usual custom. Try to be the same with the outsiders as you are within your group.

Your learnings about yourself, about cross-culture interaction, and about culture itself will be enhanced to the extent that you can behave in this manner.

Your group task for this period is to discuss this matter fully so that these norms become a part of you. You may wish to practice them with the use of role playing, or you may suggest additional supporting behaviors such as signs and symbols for use between yourselves.

FORM YOUR OWN CULTURE

Green Group

Your group task for the next hour or so is to **form your own culture**. The task for the other group during this time is the same. At the end of this planning period, you are invited to an Embassy Reception where your group and the other can meet together and get acquainted.

A culture is the totality of the norms, standards, and behaviors that operate in a society. These attributes distinguish a society's members, individually and collectively, from other societies and cultures. The Cultural Universals handout will assist you to develop your own distinct culture. You will heighten your uniqueness as a culture if you maintain the following ground rules:

1. When you are interacting with a member of your own group, be as open, spontaneous, and helpful as you can. Both give and seek support from your group members, whether you are alone with them or in the presence of outsiders.

2. When interacting with members of the other group, do everything you can to learn as much about them as possible. Inquire, express interest, and show curiosity about them as individuals and as a group. Be supportive of them.

3. When interacting with the other group, however, **reveal nothing about yourself, either as an individual or as a culture.** It is a fixed moral code of the Greens not to divulge any personal or group information.

Your learnings about yourself, about cross-culture interaction, and about culture itself will be enhanced to the extent that you can behave in this manner.

Your group task for this period is to discuss this matter fully so that these norms become a part of you. You may wish to practice with the use of role playing, or you may suggest additional supporting behaviors such as signs and symbols for use between yourselves.

CONCEPTS SHAPING THE AMERICAN WAY OF LIFE

1. **Action is good.**
   Change can be induced through individual or group action. "Getting things done" is commendable. Problems, once identified, can be solved.

2. **Man's environment can be controlled.**
   Nature is to be conquered and made over to suit man's needs.

3. **Progress is straight-lined and upward, not spiral.**
   Change is inevitable and Utopia is the result of achievement and progress.

4. **The material is more real than the spiritual.**
   The concrete and observable are relevant. Material comfort and convenience are emphasized.

5. **A person's success is self-made.**
   Social status accrues to one who succeeds in the face of competition.

6. **The individual is the keystone of society.**
   Individual responsibility is important, and "the greatest good for the greatest number" leads to a successful society. Minority rights must be protected.

7. **Man is a moral creature.**
   Personal conduct can be evaluated in universal moral terms. Clearcut ethical distinctions can be made that affect all people equally.

8. **Time is money.**
   Time is a material thing. It should be actively mastered or manipulated to one's advantage.

9. **The world is rational.**
   Scientific reasoning is the unquestioned way of understanding the physical world.

10. **The American is open and friendly and so are other people when dealt with in an open and friendly way.**
    People of traditional, formal cultures often view as ill-mannered the openness, use of first names, personal questions, display of enthusiasm in public, and open displays of affection that are characteristics of Americans. Americans tend to overlook this disapproval.

CULTURAL UNIVERSALS

Even casual observation of people within the United States or abroad reveals cultural differences between ourselves and those with a different way of life. Suppose we wish to learn a culture in depth and in an organized way. If we were to want to make ourselves specialists on a foreign area and go beyond the superficial tourist observations, how would we go about it?

Below is a list of many categories of cultural traits, or universals, that have been found to be common to all cultures, past or present. These categories refer to what the people of an area both do and think. A specialist would want to study many of these categories, and a specialist in depth would watch for differences between what people say their behavior means to them and what they show it really means.

As you form your own culture in this simulation, the use of items from this list may help you to give consistency and reality to the norms you adopt. Starred items (*) may be useful as starting points for forming your culture, but do not limit yourself only to these items.

1. age grading
2. athletic sports
3. bodily adornment
4. calendar
5. cleanliness training
6. community organization
7. cooking
8. cooperative labor
9. cosmology
10. courtship
11. dancing
12. decorative art
13. divination
14. division of labor
15. dream interpretation
16. education
17. eschatology
18. ethics
19. ethnobotany
20. etiquette
21. faith healing
22. family*
23. feasting
24. fire making
25. folklore
26. food taboos
27. funeral rites
28. games
29. gestures*
30. gift giving
31. government*
32. greetings*
33. hair styles
34. hospitality
35. housing
36. hygiene
37. incest taboos
38. inheritance rules*
39. joking
40. kin groups
41. kinship nomenclature
42. language
43. law
44. luck superstitions
45. magic
46. marriage*
47. mealtimes
48. medicine
49. modesty concerning natural functions
50. mourning
51. music
52. mythology
53. numerals
54. obstetrics
55. penal sanctions
56. personal names*
57. population policy
58. postnatal care
59. pregnancy usages
60. property rites*
61. propitiation of supernatural beings
62. puberty customs
63. religious ritual*
64. residence rules
65. sexual restrictions
66. soul concepts
67. status differences
68. surgery
69. tool making
70. trade
71. visiting
72. weaning
73. weather control

This list has been adapted from George P. Murdock, "The Common Denominator of Cultures," in Ralph Linton (Ed.), **The Science of Man in the World Crisis**, Columbia University Press, 1945, pp. 123-142. Used with permission.

27 Intergroup Collaboration: A Cross-Cultural Experience

Purposes

I. To engage in a collaborative enterprise in the face of intergroup barriers.

II. To analyze and generalize the experience for application to intercultural situations.

Group Size

Participants work in separate groups of seven to fifteen members each.

Time Required

One and one-half hours.

Setting

This activity fits well into a race-relations training program, or it can follow activity 26, "A Cross-Cultural Experience," for a program on intercultural relations. The best setting is a meeting room that can be divided in the middle by a sliding partition or a screen, which is kept closed until step VII of the Procedure. One group works on each side of the screen. Short of these accommodations, the group can work on either side of a long table that is tipped on its side, or a screen may be made of blankets. Another room is required for periodic "communication meetings," in which the two groups meet together.

Materials

I. Two boxes of Tinkertoys.™

II. Notepaper and pencils for each group.

III. Two yardsticks or rulers.

IV. A copy of the appropriate Language Instruction Sheet for each member of Group A and of Group B.

V. A large display copy of the Time Schedule.

Procedure

I. Introduce the activity as follows:

A. You are divided into two groups that represent different countries. You can name your own country if you like. Your countries are divided by a river. Your governments have agreed to collaborate in building a bridge across the river with a construction crew starting from each side. You are the construction crews. Here are your bridge-building materials. (Give each group an unopened box of Tinkertoys.)

B. Because of conditions of continuous dense fog, you cannot see the other side of the river. The screen represents the lack of visibility.

C. Your task is to build a bridge so that it will meet exactly in the center of the river, coming together with a good fit. Naturally, the elegance of your bridge design will reflect favorably on your country.

D. You will have opportunities to communicate in joint meetings, which I will tell you about later. We will be following this schedule (display the following time schedule on a flipchart):

TIME SCHEDULE

Introduction and instructions	10 minutes
Construction	45 minutes
Organizing	5 minutes
Communication meeting	5 minutes
Construction	5 minutes
Communication meeting	5 minutes
Construction	10 minutes
Communication meeting	5 minutes
Construction	5 minutes
Process period	35 minutes

E. We will begin by closing the screen and giving you five minutes to get yourselves organized, become familiar with your construction materials, and appoint a person to represent you in the first intergroup communication session.

II. Close the screen or otherwise separate the two groups and allow them five minutes to organize themselves.

III. While they are getting themselves organized, visit each of the groups in turn and hand out their respective Language Instruction Sheets with the following instructions:

Since you are from different countries you naturally speak different languages, but you have learned English and you will speak in English at the communication meeting. However, there are three words that give you trouble. They are listed on your Language Instruction Sheet. During the communication meeting, be sure that you use these words as instructed when they come up in your conversation.

IV. Call both groups together in another room for a communication meeting and announce the following ground rules:

A. Communication representatives sit in the center. All others may observe and, if you like, take notes.

B. Observers may not interrupt the meeting in any way.

C. This meeting is limited to five minutes.

D. Communication representatives may talk about anything they choose. Their common goal, of course, is to make the center of the bridge come together with a good fit when the partition is removed.

V. Allow five minutes for the communication meeting. Then the groups return to their respective sides of the screen and proceed with construction. Caution: Do not allow the participants to glimpse the construction of the other group as they pass to and from the communication meetings.

VI. Convene two more communication meetings according to the schedule. The groups will appoint a different person to be their representative each time. They are to follow the same language instructions.

VII. When the construction is completed, remove the screen with appropriate ceremony. It should not be until the screen is moved that the groups know whether their collaboration is successful or not.

VIII. Conduct a general sharing of process comments. This activity provides a plentiful supply of data to be examined for individual, intragroup, and intergroup learnings. For extracting learnings on the level of intergroup and cross-cultural dynamics, focus on the following points:

    A. Consider the trust issue between groups. How did trust develop?

    B. Was there a sense of rivalry and competition? What did this do to your ability to collaborate?

    C. In what ways did the language problem *enhance* the communication process?

    D. What statements of principle can we now make regarding intergroup or intercultural collaboration? (List on flipchart.)

    E. Do these principles apply to subgroups within a culture, for example, black-white relations?

LANGUAGE INSTRUCTION SHEET: GROUP A.

Whenever you mean **Short**, say the word **Long**

Whenever you mean **Up**, say the word **Down**

Whenever you mean any color, say the word **Green**

LANGUAGE INSTRUCTION SHEET: GROUP B

Whenever you mean **High**, say the word **Wide**

Whenever you mean **Top**, say the word **Side**

Whenever you mean any number, say the word **Three**

Part four
Stress Training

28 Stress: A Mental Arithmetic Experiment

Purposes

I. To produce stress in selected persons as evidenced by increased pulse rate.

II. To compare the stressors in this experimental situation with on-the-job conditions.

Group Size

Three persons are selected from a group of any size for this demonstration.

Time Required

Thirty minutes.

Materials

I. A stop watch.

II. Pencil and paper for each participant.

III. A blank flipchart and markers.

Procedure

I. Hand out a sheet of paper and a pencil to each participant. Then train all the group members to measure their pulse rate as follows:

   A. Find your pulse by lightly placing your right index and second finger on the inside of your left wrist below the base of your left thumb. Raise your hand when you have found your pulse.

   B. Has everyone found his or her pulse? Good. I want you to count your pulse for fifteen seconds. Using a stopwatch for accuracy, I will count the time for you. Start! (Fifteen seconds.) Stop! Multiply the count of your pulse by four to obtain your pulse rate per minute.

II. Ask for the highest and lowest rates in the group and record them on the flipchart. A rate of seventy-six to ninety beats per minute is in the average range. Repeat the procedure to be sure that everyone can do it, and ask everyone to do the following:

   Prepare a record of your pulse rate by listing the numbers 1 to 5 on a sheet of paper and entering your pulse rate, as follows (write the numbers on the flipchart):

   1. 76
   2.
   3.
   4.
   5.

   I am going to ask you to record your pulse rate several times, so be ready.

Part 4. Stress Training   115

III. Set up the demonstration as follows:
   A. Explain, "We are going to perform a brief experiment on pulse rates."
   B. Place three chairs up front, facing the audience.
   C. Explain, "I will select three people to do this task for us while everybody else watches. It is not a hard task, but we want them to be here where everyone can see them."
   D. Point to three participants, saying, "You, you, and you will be our demonstrators." Wait only a moment and then say, "Now, everyone, take your pulse and record it on your paper next to the number 2." Be sure that those selected for the demonstration do this, along with everyone else.
   E. Ask the demonstrators to take their seats in front of the group and bring their pulse records with them.
   F. Ask, "Now, everyone take his or her pulse again and write it on the record next to number 3."

IV. Give instructions and introduce the demonstration by saying:

   In a moment I'm going to ask you three demonstrators to subtract from 1000 by 7's. We will see who can do this the best. The rest of you observe. I will use the stop watch for accuracy. Ready? Start! (Allow twenty seconds.) Stop! Now, everyone, take your pulse and write it down next to number 4.

V. Collect data on the demonstration.
   A. Find out which of the demonstrators had subtracted the furthest, going down from 1000, and write the best scores on the flipchart. This is unimportant to the purpose of the experiment on stress, but it is often personally important to the participants, especially if some competition has developed.
   B. Ask the demonstrators for their lists of pulse rates and write them on the flipchart for comparison. Usually the number 4 pulse rates, taken immediately after the subtraction task, are the highest.
   C. Ask the members of the audience if their fourth pulse rate was also higher. In the majority it will not be.
   D. Ask everyone to take his or her pulse rate once more. Check with the demonstrators to see if their rates have subsided.

IV. Conduct a discussion to explore the following issues:
   A. Can the demonstrators explain why their pulse rates went up or did not go up? Emphasize that stressors may or may not produce stress in an individual; this depends on how the person responds in the presence of a stressor.
   B. What was the combination of stressors in this situation?
      1. A mental task of moderate difficulty.
      2. Being in front of an audience — being observed.
      3. Competition.
   C. How are these factors similar to stressors back home in the work situation?

29 Develop Your Support System

Purposes

I. To understand the need for an emotional support system.
II. To identify your present support system.
III. To develop a more complete emotional support system for yourself.

Time Required

One hour.

Setting

This activity is appropriate for a training program on the management of stress. The model is also useful in the training of managers or in human relations training programs. There is little interaction; it is primarily a presentation followed by individual application.

Materials

I. A copy of Develop Your Support System for each participant.
II. A note pad and pencil for each participant.
III. A blank flipchart and markers.

Procedure

I. Introduce the activity by presenting the following points:

A. People vary in their ability to be self-sufficient. Some individuals need other people around much of the time and others enjoy being alone much of the time.

B. The reasons why people differ in this regard are many. Their self-sufficiency may stem from their family environment and whether they were the first child, only child, or in the middle somewhere. It could be due to their early socialization in junior or senior high school. People are also influenced by their present working conditions, particularly the constellation of people they are with while working.

C. The fact is that no one is self-sufficient because we all depend on others for certain things. This can be illustrated with a short experiment. On your note pads, draw a line down the center of the page. On the left, list the names of people you need and like to have around you, or make contact with from time to time. (Five minutes.) Now on the right side, after each name, indicate what

---

This activity was developed from ideas presented by Charles Seashore during a training program in Bethel, Maine. Seashore is a consulting social psychologist in Washington, D.C.

you can count on that person for: why you like to have contact with him or her, why do you need the person? (Five minutes.)

II. Indicate to the participants that you want to get an idea of "What needs do people meet for you?" Ask them to call out items from their right-hand-column lists, while you write the items on the flipchart.

III. Review the list and show the participants that their needs fall into categories such as:

Physical needs: sex, food, shelter;

Psychological needs: caring, understanding, listening, intimacy;

Social needs: Belonging, status, group identity, helping others.

IV. Ask them to note how some people on their lists may meet several categories of need, although probably no one serves as an "all-purpose need-meeter."

V. Work further with improving the participants' understanding of a support system by discussing the following questions:

    A. How is contact made with the people on your list?
        1. By being with them at home or at work?
        2. By telephone or by letter?
    B. How often do you contact them?
        1. Every day?
        2. Once a week?
        3. A few times a year?
    C. Who initiates contact?
        1. You?
        2. The other?
        3. Chance circumstances?

VI. Explain that the intent of this session is to improve the effectiveness of individual support systems by planning a support system so that one's needs do not go unmet. Hand out Develop Your Support System and review how it is to be used:

    A. In the first column, on the left, is a list of needs that we probably all have; you may want to add to this list.

    B. In the next column, list the names of people who presently meet these needs for you. Some of them you can transfer from your previous list, and a person's name may occur after more than one of the needs. If you think of no one who meets a particular need, leave it blank.

    C. The third column is for you to use as you think of expanding your support system. Write the names of people you would like to include after the need they could meet for you. (Twenty minutes.)

VII. Open the session to a general discussion with the following questions:

    A. Did you think of other needs to add to the first column?

    B. How many of you are satisfied with your support system at present?
       How many are not, and why not?

    C. Is it necessary to inform others that they are part of your system and what needs they meet for you?

    D. The system thus far has focused on *receiving* or on getting help from others. We should also consider the other side and that is "Whom do we help?" Many of the needs we have, such as belonging, intimacy, and loneliness, can be reduced by organizing our lives to include opportunities to help others.

VIII. Instruct the participants to turn the form over, draw a line down the middle, and caption the left-hand column with the words, "Whom Do I Help?", and the right-hand column with "What Can I Do to Expand This?" Tell them they have about five minutes to list names and opportunities under those two headings.

IX. Summarize as follows:

    A. We all have emotional support systems that are networks of people who meet various needs that we have.

    B. We can expand and use these systems to reduce any pressures we feel and to enrich our lives.

    C. We can also reduce some of our needs by helping others.

DEVELOP YOUR SUPPORT SYSTEM

TYPE OF NEED & RELEVANT SUPPORT	CURRENT STATE OF MY SYSTEM	EXPANSION POSSIBILITIES

Isolation (loneliness):
   can be met by
   people who like me

Belonging:
   can be met by
   people who **are** like me

Affirmation of competence:
   can be met by
   people who know my work

Crisis or overload:
   can be met by
   foul-weather friends

Intimacy:
   can be met by
   close personal friends

Challenge:
   can be met by
   people who ask the hard
   questions

Stimulation:
   can be met by
   people who inspire and excite

_____:

_____:

30 A Stress-Management Program

Purposes

I. To identify internal and external sources of stress.

II. To develop a plan for managing stress.

III. To gain commitment to changes and activities that will be necessary to carry out the plan.

Group Size

A workshop group of fifteen to twenty-five persons.

Time Required

About forty-five minutes.

Setting

Workshops on stress and its management have become a frequent offering both for employees within an organization and for the public. At the conclusion of such a workshop, a useful device is one that summarizes the information and individualizes for each participant how he or she will use the learnings. My Program for Managing Stress is such a device. It allows time for a thoughtful review and the writing down of some plans. From this, the participants may gain increased commitment to making changes that will reduce the effects of stress in their lives.

Materials

A copy of the My Program for Managing Stress form and a pencil for each participant.

Procedure

I. Near the end of a stress-management workshop, give each participant a pencil and a copy of the My Program for Managing Stress form.

II. Explain the form as a review of the workshop and an aid for planning an individual program of stress management. Ask the participants to fill out the form and to indicate what activities they plan to do "more of" or "less of." (Thirty minutes.)

III. When the participants are finished with their plans, ask if some would like to share their plans with the group. What do they plan to do more of or less of? *Note:* Verbal sharing as well as writing a plan tends to increase commitment.

MY PROGRAM FOR MANAGING STRESS

Name _____ Date _____

SOURCES OF STRESS FOR ME

Recent Events at Work   Recent Events Away From Work

Ongoing Conditions at Work   Ongoing Conditions Away From Work

SOURCES OF STRESS WITHIN ME

In what ways do I expect too much of myself?

What do I value or believe that is different from those around me?

What am I really afraid of?

CHECK LIST OF STRESS-MANAGEMENT STRATEGIES

What I Plan To Do More Of (+) or Less Of (−)

Physical Methods

> Strenuous exercise ±
> Mild exercise ±
> Diet ±
> Muscle-tension relaxation ±
> Get a medical examination ±
> Other

Psychological Methods

> Meditation ±
> Develop an emotional support system ±
> Resolve some interpersonal conflicts ±
> Reduce Type-A behavior ±
> Reorder my values ±
> Other

Philosophical and Spiritual Methods

> Prayer ±
> Confronting death ±
> Developing a philosophy (Who Am I?) ±
> Other

Organizational Methods

> Diagnose stress in my office ±
> Use group problem-solving methods ±
> Time management ±
> Improve the work environment ±
> Arrange to do more of what I enjoy ±
> Other

ADDITIONAL NOTES

31 Type A and Type B: Check List

Purposes

I. To identify Type-A and Type-B behaviors in one's own pattern of living.

II. To recognize their significance in coronary heart disease.

III. To initiate corrective action through attitudinal adjustment.

Group Size

The participants work in teams of five or six persons. Although the total group may be any size, it usually includes from twenty to thirty participants.

Time Required

One hour.

Setting

This activity fits well into a program for stress reduction. It also can stand alone and be used as a topic for health education and preventive medicine.

Materials

I. A copy of the Habits Questionnaire and a pencil for each participant.

II. A blank flipchart and markers.

Procedure

I. Ask the participants to fill out the Habits Questionnaire.

II. When they have completed the questionnaire, write the following item numbers on the flipchart:

| 4 | 17 | 22 | 27 | 31 |
| 8 | 20 | 24 | 28 | 32 |

These items are Type-B characteristics. Anyone who marked five or more of these items is classified as Type B and may be significantly different from individuals classified as Type A. Type A's typically make up the majority of a group.

III. Form groups of five or six persons and, if possible, ensure that a Type-B person is in each group.

This check list was developed from information given in **Type A Behavior and Your Heart**, by M. Friedman and R. H. Rosenman. Copyright © 1974 by Alfred Knopf. (Reprinted as a paperback in 1975 by Fawcett World.) Used with permission. Before using this activity, facilitators should be familiar with chapters 6, 7, and 13 of that book. The research study is described on pp. 79-80.

IV. Provide a provide a brief theoretical explanation of Type-A and Type-B behavior, covering the following points:
   A. Most of the habits described in this questionnaire represent Type-A behavior. In a research study performed in 1960 (Friedman & Rosenman, 1974, pp. 79-80) and followed up during the next ten years, people who exhibited this pattern, and who were between thirty and sixty years of age, were found to be three times more likely to experience coronary heart disease in the subsequent decade.
   B. The habits described by the numbered items written on the flipchart represent the Type-B pattern. Type B people seem to be immune to heart disease, even when they often exceed the usual rules for diet, smoking, weight, and have had parents who died of coronary heart disease. Type-B people have few of the Type-A habits.
   C. It is probable that none of us qualifies as a pure Type A or Type B. Nevertheless, it will pay for each of us to take a look at these habits and determine how we can start to change in order to become more of a Type-B person.
V. Ask the group members to review the questionnaire, compare their responses, and discuss what changes they may undertake individually. (Thirty minutes.)
VI. Bring the groups back for general sharing, using the following procedure:
   A. Ask for a general report from the groups regarding their discussion.
   B. Ask the Type-B persons whether they found their habits to be as different from the others as the questionnaire suggested.
   C. Ask for some reports from individuals regarding the habits they plan to change.
VII. Summarize the activity with the following comments:
   A. It is not easy to change Type-A habits. Psychotherapy has not been shown to help, nor behavioral modification, nor other formal efforts. Change must start with each individual.
   B. When you get home, you might want to go over the questionnaire with your spouse or someone who knows you well. Since Type-A individuals typically are unaware of many of these characteristics, you may have a higher Type-A score than you gave yourself here. Furthermore, it is wise to have some help during an effort to change, and a spouse or friend can serve this purpose.
   C. Here is further motivation to change: research shows that people who reach the highest positions in an organization are usually *not* Type A, but are likely to be Type B.

HABITS QUESTIONNAIRE

Instructions: Read each item and make a check next to statements describing habits that are characteristic of you. For purposes of the questionnaire, the items are described in their extreme form, using words such as **always** or **never**. Do not be too strict and precise with your interpretation. If the description fits you in general, although not entirely, check the item.

_____ 1. I always move and walk rapidly.
_____ 2. I tend to accent key words when I am talking.
_____ 3. I eat quickly.
_____ 4. I never feel particularly impatient.
_____ 5. Sometimes people misunderstand what I say because I speed up my speech at the end of a sentence.
_____ 6. If a new gadget comes out or if I see a beautiful piece of bric-a-brac, I like to buy it.
_____ 7. I prefer football to baseball because the game moves faster.
_____ 8. I schedule my life so that I am hardly ever rushed.
_____ 9. A slow driver ahead of me really irritates me.
_____ 10. I prefer reading condensations to wading through a whole book.
_____ 11. Small talk bores me; I like to talk about things that are important to **me**.
_____ 12. I have equipment in my car for dictating letters and ideas while I drive (or if I do not, I wish I did).
_____ 13. I have to read the paper or watch the news while eating a meal.
_____ 14. I have a couple of nervous gestures or tics, but they do not bother me much.
_____ 15. When I really want to make a point, I am apt to pound on the table.
_____ 16. It is hard for me to relax and do nothing. I usually feel guilty if I do not make use of my time.
_____ 17. I am never aware of feeling hostile or just plain angry with the world.
_____ 18. The prospect of competition makes me raring to go in there and win.
_____ 19. Some of the best solutions to problems at work come to me when I am doing something else, such as playing golf or bridge.
_____ 20. I work at a steady pace without making any fuss about it.
_____ 21. People often point out things around me that I have not noticed, such as a bird, a flower, or a sunset.
_____ 22. It does not bother me a bit when I lose in a game, even if I am really pretty good at it.
_____ 23. Things often break around me, such as shoe laces, pencil points, and buttons off my clothing, or I grind my teeth.
_____ 24. I love to take a vacation and just do nothing.
_____ 25. My reports are always in on time or even before they are due; I am efficient in this respect.
_____ 26. I enjoy being one up on others, especially the people who are trying so hard to get ahead.
_____ 27. I get a lot of relaxation from sports, such as a game of tennis, handball, or swimming.
_____ 28. I prefer to talk about other things than successes I have enjoyed.
_____ 29. I cannot say no, and my schedule is usually crowded.
_____ 30. I have a long cord on my telephone so that I can walk around while I talk (or I would like to have one).
_____ 31. I can truly say that it does not bother me to be late to a meeting.
_____ 32. My philosophy is "If you miss the plane, there'll be another one soon — no need to sweat about it."

Part five
Women's Issues

32 The Pre-Employment Interview

There is a need for a training device that helps individuals to conduct pre-employment interviews without incurring complaints of discrimination. Managers and supervisors must have a clear understanding of what is required by the Equal Employment Opportunity (EEO) rules and regulations. People in personnel departments must have this understanding as a matter of course, but every manager and supervisor who interviews job candidates before hiring must be aware of areas in which even apparently innocent questions, asked in good faith, can leave the company open to costly and time-consuming charges of discrimination.

This activity is designed to be a pre-employment-interview training tool. It provides the basis for a discussion of the potential areas of inquiry in an interviewer's pre-employment contact with a job candidate. The discussion of these areas should result in a better grasp of the intent of the equal-employment-opportunity regulations and enable the participants to conduct an effective, nonbiased selection interview.

Purposes

I. To assess one's present understanding of permissable inquiries under fair employment practices.
II. To become acquainted with the basic principles of equal-employment laws through discussion of selected issues.
III. To measure at the end of the session whether such principles have been grasped.

Group Size

From fifteen to thirty people may participate, although better discussion is obtained from a group of smaller size.

Time Required

One hour.

Setting

This activity may be used in a classroom or in a roundtable seminar setting. It may be used either for an in-house training program or as a special event for managers from a variety of organizations. It could also fit into an awareness training program on male-female issues or minority issues (EEO Training Program), such as those conducted on a college campus.

Materials

I. A copy of the Pretest for Pre-Employment Inquiries and a pencil for each participant.
II. A copy of the Posttest for Pre-Employment Enquiries for each participant.
III. One copy of Guidelines for Pre-Employment Inquiries for the facilitator.

Procedure

I. Introduce the session by reviewing the following items:

   A. In order to operate their daily employment offices, businesses must comply with federal EEO laws if they:
      1. Employ fifteen persons or more;
      2. Are contracting with the government;
      3. Are covered by the Fair Labor Standards Act; or
      4. Participate in a federally subsidized program.
   B. Title VII of the 1964 Civil Rights Act bans all discrimination in employment because of race, color, religion, sex, or national origin.
   C. The Equal Pay Act of 1963 forbids pay differentials based on sex.
   D. The Age Discrimination in Employment Act bans discrimination because of age, between the ages of 40 and 70 years.
   E. The Rehabilitation Act of 1973 requires employers with government contracts to take affirmative action for qualified handicapped individuals.
   F. The intent of these laws and regulations is to broaden the opportunity for employment to many groups that formerly had been excluded. By moral imperative, employment practices should be open to anyone. Now, by law, bias must be guarded against for women, racial and religious minorities, the handicapped, and the aging.
   G. We may not be aware of some of the biases that we have. This test may help us to know more about them.

II. Hand out Pretest for Pre-Employment Inquiries and a pencil to each participant. Explain that there will be no grade, the group is going to discuss each item, participants can take notes on the test paper, and they have ten minutes to complete the test. Call time in ten minutes and then discuss each item on the test, supplying the correct answer as you do so. Discussion will be livelier if the answer is not given until after the participants have tried to reach agreement on their preferred choice. As the facilitator, you may use Guidelines for Pre-Employment Inquiries to explain the lawful and unlawful aspects for each item.

III. When all items on the Pretest have been reviewed, hand out a copy of Posttest for Pre-Employment Inquiries for completion by each participant. (Ten minutes.)

IV. When all participants have completed the Posttest, announce the correct answers and allow the participants to score their own tests. Check to see how many improved on their Pretest scores.

V. Summarize by making the following points:

   A. Inquiries that are directly related to bona fide occupational qualifications are permitted.
   B. Some inquiries that are asked of all applicants, especially of males and females alike, are permitted.
   C. No data may be required nor questions asked that may be construed as seeking information regarding racial background, religious affiliation, handicaps, or other personal information that is not reasonably related to fitness for performing the job.
   D. The job requirements should come first in your mind. Questions you may want to ask that go beyond job requirements may suggest biases. Before you ask such questions, ask yourself, "Is this something I really need to know?"

PRETEST FOR PRE-EMPLOYMENT INQUIRIES

Instructions: Read each item as though you were conducting a pre-employment interview. Ask yourself, "May I ask this question?" and indicate your answer by marking an X under "Yes" or "No." A space is provided for you to take notes on the test pages during discussion.

	YES	NO	NOTES

1. "Have you ever worked for any company under a different name?"
2. (Of a woman applicant) "How many children do you have?"
3. (Of a woman applicant) "Do you plan to start a family soon?"
4. "This job frequently requires overtime, including Saturdays. Would that be a problem for you?"
5. (Of an applicant who says he is 21, but looks younger) "We cannot hire people under the legal age. You must bring your birth certificate before we can hire you."
6. "Do you have any handicaps?"
7. (Of a male applying to work as your secretary) "I have always had a woman secretary. Do you think you would be happy in this job?"
8. "Do you have any distinguishing scars?"
9. "Do you live with relatives? What is their name?"
10. "How long have you lived at your present address?"
11. "Were you born in this country?"
12. "What training did you receive in the Army?"
13. "We need a photograph. If you are hired will you bring one for your personal file?"
14. "We would like a photo to attach to your application, since so many are applying. Would you mind supplying us with one?"
15. "Are you a citizen of the U.S.?"
16. "What language do you speak at home?"
17. "Your French is very good. Where did you learn it?"
18. "You went to St. John's Prep? What kind of school is that?"
19. "Have you ever been convicted of a crime?"
20. (Of an applicant in her late 20s) "What is your parents' address?"
21. "We need the name of a relative to be notified in case of an emergency."
22. "List the names of organizations, clubs, and lodges to which you belong."
23. "Have your wages ever been garnisheed by a credit company?"
24. "Who referred you for a position here?"
25. (Notice printed on the application form) "Any misstatements or omissions of material facts may be cause for dismissal."

POSTTEST FOR PRE-EMPLOYMENT INQUIRIES

Instructions: Read each item as though you were conducting a pre-employment interview. Ask yourself, "May I ask this question?" and indicate your answer by marking an X under "Yes" or "No."

	YES	NO
1. "That's an unusual name. What nationality is it?"	___	___
2. "Are you single, married, or divorced?"	___	___
3. "Do you plan to move from this community any time soon?"	___	___
4. (Of an applicant who is a minor) "Do you have a work permit?"	___	___
5. "This job requires you to be on your feet a lot. Do you have any physical condition that we should know about in considering your application?"	___	___
6. "I notice that you were limping as you came in. What is the problem?"	___	___
7. (Of a woman applicant) "This job requires a lot of heavy lifting. Do you think that you can do it?"	___	___
8. "You look like you had an American Indian ancestor. Am I right?"	___	___
9. "Do you own your home or are you renting?"	___	___
10. "I notice that you lived in France. Were your parents born there?"	___	___
11. "Where have you lived during the last five years?"	___	___
12. "What is your church affiliation?"	___	___
13. (Of an applicant with a "Jewish" name) "Do you observe Kosher rules in eating?"	___	___
14. "Did you receive an honorable discharge from the Army?"	___	___
15. "We like to have a photo with the application but it's not required. Would you like to send us one?"	___	___
16. (Of a naturalized citizen) "If you are hired, we will need proof of citizenship. Could you then supply us with copies of your naturalization papers?"	___	___
17. "Do you have fluency in any foreign language?"	___	___
18. "List the schools you have attended."	___	___
19. "We have a company training program for this job, and everyone takes it, but do you already have experience related to it?"	___	___
20. "Have you ever been arrested?"	___	___
21. (Of a minor) "What is the address of your parent or guardian?"	___	___
22. "Who should be notified in case of emergency?"	___	___
23. "Some of the organizations you belong to are listed by initials only. What do they stand for?"	___	___
24. "Have you ever had trouble obtaining credit?"	___	___
25. "Please include the name of your pastor or minister among your references."	___	___

THE PRE-EMPLOYMENT INTERVIEW SCORING KEYS

PRETEST

1. Yes
2. No
3. No
4. Yes
5. No
6. No
7. No
8. Yes
9. No
10. Yes
11. No
12. Yes
13. Yes
14. No
15. Yes
16. No
17. No
18. No
19. No
20. No
21. No
22. No
23. No
24. Yes
25. Yes

POSTTEST

1. No
2. No
3. Yes
4. Yes
5. Yes
6. Yes
7. No
8. No
9. No
10. No
11. Yes
12. No
13. No
14. No
15. No
16. Yes
17. Yes
18. Yes
19. No
20. No
21. Yes
22. Yes
23. No
24. No
25. No

GUIDELINES FOR PRE-EMPLOYMENT INQUIRIES

	LAWFUL INQUIRIES	**UNLAWFUL INQUIRIES**
Name	"Have you worked for this organization under a different name? Is any additional information relative to change of name or use of an assumed name or nickname necessary to enable a check on your work and educational record? If yes, explain."	Inquiries about the name which would indicate applicant's lineage, ancestry, national origin, or descent. Inquiries into previous name of applicant where it has been changed by court order, marriage, or otherwise.
Marital and Family Status	Whether applicant can meet specified work schedules or has activities, commitments, or responsibilities that may hinder the meeting of work attendance requirements. Inquiries as to a duration to stay on job or anticipated absences, which are made to males and females alike.	Any inquiries indicating whether an applicant is married, single, divorced, engaged, etc. Number and age of children. Any questions concerning pregnancy. Any such question which directly or indirectly results in limitation of job opportunity in any way.
Age	If a minor, require proof of age in form of a work permit or a certificate of age. Require proof of age by birth certificate after being hired. Inquiry as to whether or not the applicant meets the minimum age requirements as set by law and requirements that upon hire, proof of age must be submitted. If age is a legal requirement: "If hired, can you furnish proof of age?"; or statement that hire is subject to verification of age.	Requirement that applicant produce proof of age in the form of a birth certificate or baptismal record.
Handicaps	Whether applicant has any handicaps or health problems, — sensory, mental, or physical — which may affect work performance or which the employer should consider in determining job placement.	General inquiries (i.e., "Do you have any handicaps?") which would tend to divulge handicaps or health conditions which do not relate reasonably to fitness to perform the job.
Sex	Inquiry or restriction of employment is permissible only where a bona fide occupational qualification exists. (This BFOQ exception is interpreted very narrowly by the courts and EEOC.) The burden of proof rests on the employer to prove that the BFOQ does exist and that all members of the affected class are incapable of performing the job.	Sex of the applicant. Any other inquiry which would indicate sex. Sex is not a BFOQ because a job involves physical labor (such as heavy lifting) beyond the capacity of some women nor can sex be used as a factor for determining whether or not an applicant will be satisfied in a particular job.

This chart, compiled by Clifford Coen, University of Tennessee, was originally published in the December 1976 newsletter of the American Association for Affirmative Action. It is intended for guidance only. The courts, EEOC, and state or local fair employment practice agencies may differ considerably in their interpretations of what constitutes an unlawful inquiry.

Race or Color	General distinguishing physical characteristics such as scars, etc.	Applicant's race. Color of applicant's skin, eyes, hair, etc. or other questions directly or indirectly indicating race or color. Applicant's height or weight where it is not relevant to job.
Address or Duration of Residence	Applicant's address. Inquiry into place and length of current and previous addresses: "How long a resident of this state or city?"	Specific inquiry into foreign addresses which would indicate national origin. Names or relationship of persons with whom applicant resides. Whether applicant owns or rents home.
Birthplace	After employment: "Can you submit a birth certificate or other proof of U.S. citizenship?"	Birthplace of applicant. Birthplace of applicant's parents, spouse, or other relatives. Requirement that applicant submit a birth certificate, naturalization, or baptismal record before employment. Any other inquiry to indicate or identify denomination or customs.
Military Record	Type of education and experience in service as it relates to a particular job.	Type of discharge.
Photograph	May be required after hiring for identification.	Request photograph before hiring. Requirement that applicant affix a photograph to his application. Request that applicant, at his option, submit photograph. Requirement of photograph after interview but before hiring.
Citizenship	"Are you a citizen of the U.S.? If you are not a U.S. citizen, have you the legal right to remain permanently in the U.S.? Do you intend to remain permanently in the U.S.? If not a citizen, are you prevented from lawfully becoming employed because of visa or immigration status?" Statement that if hired, applicant may be required to submit proof of citizenship.	"Of what country are you a citizen?" Whether applicant or his parents or spouse are naturalized or native-born U.S. citizens. Date when applicant or parents or spouse acquired U.S. citizenship. Requirement that applicant produce his naturalization papers or first papers. Whether applicant's parents are citizens of the U.S.
Ancestry or National Origin	Languages applicant reads, speaks, or writes fluently.	Inquiries into applicant's lineage, ancestry, national origin, descent, birthplace, or mother tongue. National origin of applicant's parents or spouse.
Education	Applicant's academic, vocational, or professional education; school attended. Inquiry into language skills such as reading, speaking, and writing foreign languages.	Inquiry asking specifically the nationality, racial, or religious affiliation of a school. Inquiry as to what is mother tongue or how foreign language ability was acquired.
Experience	Applicant's work experience. Other countries visited.	

Conviction, Arrest and Court Record	Inquiry into actual convictions which relate reasonably to fitness to perform a particular job. (A conviction is a court ruling where the party is found guilty as charged. An arrest is merely the apprehending or detaining of the person to answer the alleged crime.)	Any inquiry relating to arrests. To ask or check into a person's arrest, court, or conviction record if not substantially related to functions and responsibilities of the prospective employment.
Relatives	Names of applicant's relatives already employed by this company. Names and addresses of parents or guardian of minor applicant.	Name or address of any relative of adult applicant.
Notice in Case of Emergency	Names of persons to be notified.	Name and address of relative to be notified in case of accident or emergency.
Organizations	Inquiry into the organization of which an applicant is a member providing the name or character of the organization does not reveal the race, religion, color, or ancestry of the membership. What offices are held, if any?	"List all organizations, clubs, societies, and lodges to which you belong." The names of organizations to which the applicant belongs if such information would indicate through character or name the race, religion, color, or ancestry of the membership.
Credit Rating	None	Any questions concerning credit rating, charge accounts, etc.
References	"By whom were you referred for a position here?" Names of persons willing to provide professional and/or character references for applicant. Who suggested that applicant apply for a position here?	Require the submission of a religious reference. Request reference from applicant's pastor.
Miscellaneous	Notice to applicants that any misstatement or omissions of material facts in the application may be cause for dismissal.	

33 Promoting Women

Purposes

I. To examine women's attitudes toward promotion and the problems they may encounter when promoted.

II. To examine one's own stereotypes about women in the workplace.

Group Size

From twelve to twenty participants.

Time Required

One hour.

Setting

This activity is particularly useful in the training of supervisors and managers, and it also can be used with employees in a group session on equal employment opportunities. The group can be all male, all female, or sexually mixed. The facilitator should be highly aware of sexism in the workplace.

Materials

A copy of Promoting Women, Cases 1, 2, 3, and 4, and a pencil for each participant.[1]

Procedure

I. Hand out pencils and copies of Promoting Women, Cases 1, 2, 3, and 4, and ask the participants to read the cases carefully, writing notes, if they wish, on the case margins. Indicate that the cases will be discussed with analysis focused on the following elements:

A. Forces in the person that lead to the problem;
B. Forces around the person that lead to the problem;
C. Possible action steps for short-range and long-range change.

II. Allow ten minutes for the participants to read the cases, then open the discussion, taking each case in turn. As facilitator, your task is helping the participants to perceive their own biases regarding:

A. Women as bosses or supervisors;
B. Backlash by management in the face of women reluctant to be promoted when management is "trying to implement EEO policy";

---

[1] These cases were developed by Elizabeth Wales, Ph.D., Department of Psychiatry, Wright State University School of Medicine, Dayton, Ohio.

C. Sexism in job roles;
D. The plight of the token representative;
E. Self-interest *versus* what "others expect of me";
F. The male network and its effect on women managers.

III. The facilitator should not attempt to control or direct the discussion, or limit it strictly to the cases that are provided. This session should be regarded as basic awareness training rather than as a means of learning certain principles of management. The learning goals will have been achieved if participants have experienced some degree of self-disclosure and confrontation on issues of sexism in the workplace.

PROMOTING WOMEN, CASE 1: SARAH HILLIARD

You work in the personnel division of a large public relations firm. Yesterday, one of your colleagues came into your office to ask your advice on how to handle what he felt was a disturbing situation.

He had received a note indicating that Sarah Hilliard, an administrative assistant had refused a promotion to assistant literary promoter. He could not remember the last time anyone had refused a promotion (particularly one like this, which involved a considerable raise and higher status).

When he spoke with the employee, she was very reluctant to explain why she did not want the promotion. He sensed that she did want more responsible work, she simply did not want this particular promotion. After repeated inquiries, Sarah finally opened up. This is what she said:

> Mr. Oslo, I just don't want to work for a woman. I have nothing personal against Mrs. Delavina. I really don't know anything about her but I just don't think I'd be happy working for a woman. I had a woman supervisor once when I worked in a typing pool and I really didn't like it. I can't bear someone breathing down my neck and making all kinds of petty changes and comments. Besides I don't think she'd have confidence in me and I wouldn't have enough freedom. It's kind of hard to explain; it's just a whole bunch of small things. I just think I'd have a better chance for a good rating and another promotion if I worked for a man.

Dick was disturbed on several counts. He felt that since Sarah had been offered the promotion, she was probably ready to move up and he did not want her to become a dissatisfied employee or to look for a job in another company. On a broader scale, however, he was concerned about the long range effects of moving capable women into management positions.

"After all," he said, "if women don't want to work for other women, how can we promote on the basis of merit alone? Why do you think Sarah feels this way? I just don't know what to do about this. What do you think?"

PROMOTING WOMEN, CASE 2: KAREN JONES

Karen Jones is the supervisor of the typing pool in a large company. She has been quite successful at choosing her staff and motivating them to produce prompt, accurate work. As a result, the unit has taken on some very important work from the top executives.

This week, Karen is interviewing for an opening on her staff. She frequently does this because the people on her staff often move up to executive secretarial positions, which pleases her very much. She feels that she performs a dual service by running an efficient typing pool while simultaneously training the future secretaries of the company.

Surprisingly, she receives an application from Tom Fromm, the mail clerk whose area includes the typing pool. Karen knows Tom fairly well and has always found him pleasant, competent, and willing to extend himself when important items had to be delivered quickly. She cannot believe that he seriously meant to apply for a job as a typist, but in scanning his application, she notes that he can type fifty words per minute and had several courses in office skills in high school.

Karen is anxious to help Tom. She thinks that he would never be happy being the only man working in a typing pool. She calls her friend, Jim Ryan (manager of a large department in the company), and asks him to see if there is anything he can do for Tom.

A few days later, Karen has filled the vacancy on her staff and Tom (on Karen's recommendation) has been hired as an accounting clerk in Jim Ryan's department. Karen is satisfied that she handled the situation well and she is pleased that she was able to help Tom get a start in the company.

PROMOTING WOMEN, CASE 3: FRAN BERGSTROM

Fran has been a file clerk for Mergel and Son for twenty-five years. She works with twenty other women in a large filing section. The section is arranged by teams, four women and one supervisor to a team. Fran is the supervisor of Team B. She is liked and respected by those who work for her and has frequently been given the "problem clerks" because they could not get along with the other supervisors. Fran eats lunch with the other supervisors, all of whom agree that she does two days' work in one and still maintains a sunny disposition.

Fran does not mind working hard and she likes her work. She finds it gratifying to see the incoming baskets all empty and neatly arranged at the end of the day, and she takes pride in the correctness of the files under her supervision.

Mergel and Son has just begun an Affirmative Action Program for Women. As a result of Fran's outstanding performance and seniority, she was assigned to attend several company training programs and offered a promotion to section supervisor.

Everyone in the section encouraged Fran. They were glad to see her getting some recognition, and they thought that she would make an excellent boss. The other supervisors said that they were "glad that a woman was finally going to get some recognition and that the company was not going to bring in some college kids from the outside again."

Fran was delighted that everyone thought so highly of her, but she was not totally enthusiastic about the prospect of the new job. It required much more overtime than her present job, and it meant that she would have to rate all of her old friends and be responsible for their raises.

After thinking it over, Fran really did not think she wanted to be the section supervisor. There was a great deal to learn, she would have to work harder and longer, she would be cut off from her old friends, and the pay increase was not all that great. Even though she was not sure that she wanted the job, Fran was afraid to talk with her manager about it. She felt that she would be disappointing everyone because they were expecting her to succeed. If she turned down the job, her manager might decide that he was right about women all along, and then she would ruin it for everyone. Fran decided to take the job and do the best she could.

PROMOTING WOMEN CASE 4: ELIZABETH STEWART

Ten months ago, Elizabeth Stewart became the first woman manager in Department A. At the time of her promotion, she had been with the company for eight years, rising steadily through the supervisory ranks, outperforming her male colleagues at every level.

Elizabeth had learned during her eight-year climb that to earn a promotion, she had to far exceed the standard set for her male peers. Feeling uncomfortable socializing with the male supervisors and not wanting to be thought of as "one of the girls," she kept mostly to herself.

When Elizabeth became the first woman on a five-person management team, she felt she had finally been recognized as a competent person and that the man/woman factor would no longer be relevant.

During her first month on the job, Elizabeth became somewhat disenchanted. She still felt uncomfortable with her fellow managers. Their social conventions did not include her and as a result she missed vital bits of information, receiving it a day later in a formal memo. Meetings were disastrous for her. Her suggestions were either totally disregarded or picked up and credited to one of her male colleagues. She began to feel like something of a nonperson.

However, Elizabeth was highly motivated. She had succeeded against the odds many times before and she intended to do so again, not only for herself, but for the many women managers she hoped would follow. Not accustomed to being a team player and receiving little encouragement from the other managers, Elizabeth withdrew and worked harder. She accumulated and analyzed facts, made decisions carefully, kept to herself, and avoided errors at all costs. The costs became high: irritability, frustration, and above all the increased sense of isolation.

34 Sexism: Discussion Topics

Purposes

I. To clarify the meanings of sexism and sexual stereotyping in the world of work.

II. To uncover prejudices and increase awareness of male and female stereotypes.

Group Size

From eight to twenty persons.

Time Required

One hour or more for each discussion topic, depending on the vitality of the group.

Setting

Discussion groups dealing with women's issues take place in many settings in the consciousness-raising and problem-solving climate of today's society. The discussion topics presented here are appropriate for use in an organizational program for the improvement of EEO practices, in a college psychology or sociology class, in a church group meeting, or as part of a human relations training program. All that is needed is a group that starts with a mild interest or concern about equality and women and a trainer with a moderate background knowledge of sexism and sexist stereotyping. Groups typically develop high energy and high affect when dealing with these topics. The group may be either single sex or composed of both male and female participants.

Materials

I. A copy of each handout needed for the discussions (see procedures for each topic) and a pencil for each participant.

II. A blank flipchart, markers, and masking tape.

SEXISM DISCUSSION TOPIC: NINE CHARACTERISTICS

Procedure

I. Ask the participants to form two groups and to position their chairs so that the groups face one another. Label one group the Pros and the other group the Cons.

II. Give each participant a copy of Nine Characteristics That Women Must Have to Become a High Level Executive and a pencil and offer the following instructions:

These topics were contributed by Elizabeth Wales, Ph.D., Department of Psychiatry, Wright State University School of Medicine, Dayton, Ohio.

- The Pros should read the list with the intention of arguing *for* each statement.
- The Cons should read the list with the intention of arguing *against* each statement.
- You will have five minutes to jot down notes, such as myths, anecdotes, logic, etc., that will improve your ability to enter into the discussion.

III. After five minutes open the interaction with this cautionary statement:

We want to have a discussion, not simply a recitation of arguments. This means that you should listen, as well as speak, and answer arguments, as well as present arguments. After about five minutes on each item, we will take a vote. At that time, vote as you truly believe and feel, not from your Pro or Con position. Now let's start with the first characteristic.

IV. Allow the discussion to proceed. Some items may require more time than others. As the discussion dies down with each item, call for a vote and tally it on a flipchart.

V. Draw the discussion to a close by focusing the group on the following:

A. What effect has this discussion had on your feelings and attitudes about women in management?

B. How many of you felt comfortable in being on the side you were given — the Pro or the Con. Why?

C. What are the implications of these nine characteristics for high level *male* executives?

NINE CHARACTERISTICS THAT WOMEN MUST HAVE TO BECOME A HIGH LEVEL EXECUTIVE

1. An unrealistic degree of self-confidence.
2. An ability to handle loneliness.
3. The need to win.
4. The ability to be self-reliant in one's own self-confidence.
5. An authority problem (i.e., have difficulty accepting others having authority over oneself).
6. A proper degree of distrust of others.
7. A need for power over others.
8. An ability to become emotionally aloof from any person at any point in time.
9. A willingness to sacrifice family and friends for business.

SEXISM DISCUSSION TOPIC: WOMEN WORKING FOR WOMEN

Procedure

I. Ask the participants to write ten answers to the following question:

Why do women *not* want to work for other women?

II. When they have completed their answers to the question, go around the group and ask each person to give one reason from his or her list. Ask a participant to write them on the flipchart. Continue going around until no one has a new reason to give. Hang the sheets of the flipchart up where all all can see. (The answers will sometimes cover several sheets.)

III. Ask the group, "Which of these reasons are valid?" This will lead to considerable discussion. As the group reaches something like a consensus on various items, place a star by those considered "valid" and leave the others blank.

IV. Ask the group, "Why do you suppose these reasons that we decided are not valid were given?" Again, allow free discussion. The answers can often be summarized as due to individual experience, exceptions to the rule, and prejudicial thinking or stereotyping.

V. Ask the following questions:

- Now let's go back to the reasons we thought were valid. How can women overcome them?
- Is there anything that men can or should do to help women overcome any of these?

VI. Discussion can close with a summary given by the facilitator or by the participants. The important lessons will vary according to the group and its particular needs. For instance, women who *are* bosses may have gained insights for themselves; men may have achieved a better understanding of the problems women encounter in leadership positions; others may have become aware of their own prejudicial thinking.

SEXISM DISCUSSION TOPIC: THE CASE OF BILL AND LAURA

Procedure

I. Hand out The Case of Bill and Laura to each participant.

II. When all have read it, ask, "How would you have handled this incident if you were Laura?" Allow the group to explore the case fully.

III. After the case discussion dies down, move into dealing with the issue at a more personal level by asking participants to relate a similar incident from their own experience. (Both males and females can usually do this.) Then ask, "How would you prefer to have handled it?"

IV. Summarize with the following comments on sexism:

   A. Sexism is the systematic exclusion of women from positions of political and economic power. It is similar to racism, which has been and continues to be based on a false assumption of inferiority.

   B. Males, and especially white males, tend to define women's "natural" roles in terms of their reproductive ability rather than their wider range of human talents and contributions.

   C. A fundamental and institutional change is taking place as increasing numbers of people in the excluded groups (black people, women, and more recently, other groups such as Hispanic people) know that failure to achieve in the system is related to the structure of the system, not to their so-called personal defects.

THE CASE OF BILL AND LAURA

Characters

Bill is the top salesman for his publishing firm. He is aggressive, outgoing, friendly — a "real man's man." Laura is Bill's secretary — competent and attractive. She handles all home-office dealings with Bill's clients when he is on the road. She is a pleasant and friendly person.

A Conversation Between Bill and Laura

Bill is returning to his office after a meeting with his boss, Joe Franklin.

Bill: Laura, come in for a moment, will you?

Laura: Right away.

Bill: Let's take care of some of this correspondence while I'm in for a few days.

Laura: All right. Let me get the . . .

Bill: You know, I'm so annoyed at Joe, I just can't think.

Laura: What's wrong?

Bill: Well, he wants to bring in some high-class broad to take over Flynn's territory when he retires. I mean, I have nothing against women, as you well know — but selling — no way! I can just see the guys' faces when this dame swings in with her new line. Maybe she can sell — who knows? But a woman can't sell books to men — not these guys, anyway. I just can't understand why women won't stay where they belong. They've got it made! A guy works hard to give them what they want and they spit in his face! I just don't get it. Thank goodness **you're** not like that, Laura. I really appreciate what you do here and I'm sorry I blew up at you. It's certainly not your fault that some women want to be men and take over.

35 Presenting Yourself: Skill Training for Women

Purposes

I. To experience the selling of your ideas and opinions to others in a competitive situation.

II. To receive feedback on the manner in which you present yourself.

Group Size

This activity can be done in small groups of six or seven persons, four of whom will play the role of staff members making a presentation. The other group members will be observers and evaluators.

Time Required

One and one-half hours.

Setting

This activity can be used for in-service training in any organization. It is intended for use with an all-woman group of participants. Several groups can work at the same time. The room should be large enough to separate groups of seven persons so that the groups will not disturb one another.

Materials

I. Four participants in each group receive a Candidate Description for the four staff-member roles.

II. A copy of the Presenting Yourself Instructions for each participant.

III. A copy of the Presentation Evaluation form and a pencil for each observer.

IV. A copy of the Self-Evaluation form and a pencil for each presenter.

Procedure

I. Introduce the activity with the following information:

This activity is designed to give people practice in selling their ideas to others. Most women need experience with competitive situations in which the outcome depends to some extent on how they think on their feet and offer convincing opinions to others. Here is a safe place to practice these skills and evaluate your performance from the feedback you will receive from observers.

This activity was adapted from materials provided by Elizabeth Wales, Ph.D., Department of Psychiatry, Wright State University School of Medicine, Dayton, Ohio.

II. Arrange the participants in groups of six or seven and ask each group to choose four members to "present a case for the promotion of a candidate to a better position." Indicate that the remaining two or three in each group will be given the task of making observations and evaluations.

III. Give a copy of the Presenting Yourself Instructions to all participants and allow them time to read the instructions. Then give a Candidate Description to each presenter and a copy of the Presentation Evaluation form and a pencil to the observers.

IV. Announce the starting time and that the presentations should begin within the groups in fifteen minutes.

V. When the final rankings of the candidates have been made, about sixty-five minutes from the starting time, give a copy of the Self-Evaluation form and a pencil to each presenter and ask the group to allow them about five minutes to make notes on this form.

VI. Ask the evaluators to engage in a discussion with the presenters, giving feedback and comparing their recommendations with the presenters' self-evaluations. (Twenty minutes.)

VII. To summarize, ask for reports from the groups on "What impressed you in this experience, and what did you learn from it?"

CANDIDATE DESCRIPTION 1: BILL JOHNSON

Bill Johnson is a staff assistant with nine years' total service with the company. He is thirty-three years old. Bill is attending night school, taking a course in business management. He is interested in church work and is involved in many projects at his church. He is the same way in the office, too. You always know what Bill is doing, both at the church and on the job. When he completes assignments, it is evident that he takes pride in his accomplishments. He does not bore you with self-praise, but lets you know how things are going, what problems are encountered, and how they have been solved. He is a good man for this type of work. He is clean in manner and speech and is a good representative of his church and his company. There is not a company function that Bill does not try to attend, and when he does, he has a good time.

On the job, Bill can be counted on to turn in accurate and complete reports covering his operations. He understands what his responsibilities are and does everything he can to fulfill them. These two things seem to tie together. When you read his reports, they are right to the point and they are clear, concise, and provide a good picture of his operations.

Bill's group is the kind that gets a lot of work done and does it without incurring overtime. For the past year now, his group has come up as the best performing group in the office, although it is not made up of any particularly specialized or skilled people.

Several weeks ago, there was a special audit that had to be conducted at the office. The accounting people requested the information and also requested that the staff assistants conduct the check. This caused quite a furor among the staff assistants. Several of them gave the manager a bad time about how busy they were, etc. Bill and a couple of other fellows took it in stride. Bill almost always carries out assignments without back talk or arguments. He questions in order to understand, but not to resist taking on the job. There is an odd thing about Bill. He takes these things in stride and is good natured, but after the jobs are completed, he is prone to complain about how hard he has to work. When this audit was completed, he was telling a group of the other staff assistants that he felt he worked too hard. All these special jobs, his involvement in church work, his continuing effort toward a good record, all seem to him to add up to working too hard. He told his manager these things, too. He also is frank with his manager on other things, such as the training of new people, the promotion of his people, etc. He does not hold anything back from his manager, but, at the same time, he does not burden the boss with a lot of petty details.

Another thing that is evident, both in Bill's day-to-day performance and off the job, is the way he is perfectly at ease when meeting new people. The other week, the manager had several employee relations representatives in the office and was showing them around. When they came to Bill's desk, he was perfectly at ease and did not run around looking important, trying to impress the visitors. When they came into the office, he walked over, was introduced by the manager to the visitors, indicated he was glad to meet them, and then simply said, "May I help you in any way?" As he explained the policies, it seemed that he had known these people all his life.

CANDIDATE DESCRIPTION 2: SUSAN JONES

Susan Jones has been a staff assistant for the past four years and has a total of eleven years' service with this company. She is thirty-six years old. She is the kind of person who can keep calm even though the pressure is on. This may be due to her training in the Army. Several weeks ago, when her work was behind schedule, a meeting was called that required all attending to prepare compensation statistics prior to the meeting. Susan obtained all the necessary material and worked late until all the work was done. She worked calmly and did not go to pieces.

Susan is taking personnel courses at the university at night. She is the kind of person who is anxious to get ahead. She feels the courses have helped to order her thinking regarding her approach to people. One of the courses she is taking at the university, personnel management, is directly tied in with her work, but another course, business economics, is not directly applicable. However, Susan wants to learn all she can about business and is looking forward to using her new knowledge in the future.

Susan's work is complicated because of the many different plans she is responsible for interpreting. In addition, special procedures are being tested in her section, which require a lot of paper work. There is a problem with these reports: Susan makes the same mistakes each month on one of them. The other day the manager had to check this error again. It is not an intentional thing, and Susan admits her mistakes. She said it was her error and that she would take care of it.

When Susan comes into the office in the morning or after lunch, she starts work immediately. There is no fooling around, talking, or visiting. She feels that if people are not always on time, it can very easily hold up other sections. Susan is aware of this and knows how her job affects the overall company image.

Susan is an even-tempered person. When she was appointed, a man in her section thought he should have had her job. When Susan started her job, this fellow started to needle her, tantalize her, and try to upset her. It was like a one-man hate campaign. Susan handled this situation well. She did not blow up, as she well could have. This fellow even tried to "get Susan's goat" by criticizing the way she dressed. This did not work because Susan dresses for the job and all the people in the group knew that.

Several months ago, a new copying system was scheduled to be installed. Several months of planning were required involving sales personnel and engineers. Several weeks prior to the installation, the sales representatives came to the office and explained the installation procedure to Susan. As they proceeded through the procedure step by step, Susan had to point out several things that they had overlooked. A couple of the items that they had missed were rather serious. The others were of a lesser nature, but important enough that the system design had to be changed to meet the problems Susan recognized.

CANDIDATE DESCRIPTION 3: ROBERTA SMITH

Roberta Smith is thirty years old. She has been a staff assistant for the past three years and has been with this company for ten years. She is active in church work and, among other things, is the leader of a Girl Scouts troop.

Roberta is the kind of person who can handle more than one thing at a time. There was a situation in her office not too long ago when the manager was out sick. A big job involving a number of type changes was pending. This change involved other sections as well as her own. The manager asked her to coordinate the work, which she did, and she still kept her own job going. She has worked on other special assignments and seems able to fit them into her work schedule.

There was the time at lunch when Roberta happened to overhear a couple of her co-workers talking to some people from another section. Her co-workers were telling the others about a new plan for dispensing compensation and benefits information they were trying out and how well the method was working. The others indicated they would like to try it, but, according to them, their section was always left out. Roberta knew differently, but she thought someone should coordinate the various trials of new techniques with all the sections so that they all would be informed and keep their people informed. She suggested to her manager that this be done. Her manager asked her if she would like to take on the responsibility. Roberta took over with her usual cheerful approach and got the project under way.

Another time, Roberta was given a job to be worked into the normal operation of her job. It was a new task to her, and before jumping in, she started asking questions: What schedule had been set up? How was it established? What were some of the alternative considerations given before this technique was decided on? After getting the answers to these and other pertinent questions, she began to plan how she would start this job. She set up each step: the introduction to the sections, what each person's part would be, the next step, etc. This took a lot of work on Roberta's part, but she did it well and on schedule.

There is something else about Roberta that was evident not only on this job but in her everyday job. She has a group of about ten men and women with whom she deals regularly. Some are new, some have been around for ten to fifteen years, and they naturally are all different. She had one fellow who was always cynical about new policies and procedures. This fellow could have disrupted a lot of people, but Roberta observed him closely and tactfully. She talked with him at opportune times and was able to add the talks and observations together and come up with some constructive ways to deal with him. She seemed to understand how he felt about things and was able to get his cooperation.

There are some indications that Roberta may be unduly critical of people, both in her own section and in the sections with which she deals, especially when they do not meet her standards or work as hard as she does. One time, some men in another manager's group were, as Roberta called it, "goofing off." Their own manager was not in the office because he had gone home early. The next day, Roberta told the manager he should have more control over his men and would have, if he set up more rigid rules and stuck around to administer the rules.

She has worked out procedures for controlling lost time, clarifying communications, and responding to questions from other areas and, even though she develops these things on her own, she always checks them out with her manager. Roberta respects her boss, not only for his job knowledge and his position, but as a person.

CANDIDATE DESCRIPTION 4: JOHN TAYLOR

John Taylor has eleven years' service with this company, four as a staff assistant for benefits. John is active in the Civic Club and in his church. Colleagues from his own, as well as other sections, are always with him at lunch or want to be on his team. In addition to his friendliness, another reason for this might be the way John operates. The coffee break never seems to be a problem with him. When it is time for the break, he stops, takes the break, but more important, he is back to work in a few minutes.

John catches on to new things rather quickly. Last week at the corporate benefits meeting, the corporate benefits consultant explained the forthcoming announcement of a new benefit plan that would necessitate a great deal of paperwork and many explanatory meetings. In addition, a new system of monitoring the plan was being instituted and special reports would be required for several weeks. This did not bother John. He quickly understood the routine and changes. He is the same on other matters, whether administrative or technical. When he does not understand, he asks questions, not to make conversation or look good, but because the result of these questions usually has a clarifying effect for other people, too.

There are times, not only in meetings, but on the everyday job, when John readily expresses his own ideas. The other day, one of the other staff assistants was confronted with a problem on explaining a special disability program. The problem was similar to one John had experienced and the two of them started to discuss the problem. It happened that the benefits advisor was in the office and dropped by at this time. This did not bother John at all. He was very much at ease, as he always is with other managers, and continued to discuss the problem, throwing in his ideas as the conversation progressed. By this time, the other staff assistants came over, and they all joined in the discussion. Finally, one of them suggested that the problem and possible solution should be summed up, and John, using good grammar, went right ahead and did a fine job.

There is an interesting thing about John. He is very active in the Civic Club and his church, and sometimes he seems to be more interested in these activities than in the job. He has been off quite a few days and also has left work early on some occasions in order to be present at committee meetings either for the club or the church. He talks about these activities at the office, also. It seems as though he overemphasizes these activities.

Another thing that John can do is to get jobs done the way his manager wants them done. They will discuss the job, and John can sense the way his manager wants things done. John is not a "yes" man; he explores all angles, expresses his opinion, and then knows about what the boss wants. John does not easily get upset when things are going wrong. There have been several times when he could have. One of these instances involved a fire in the office that destroyed crucial references. John promptly arranged to have replacements reproduced and delivered. All the staff assistants had replacement copies the next day.

PRESENTING YOURSELF INSTRUCTIONS

This activity is designed to see how well you can present your point of view on a problem. The problem is to present the case for a candidate being considered for promotion within your company. For this activity, consider yourself a compensation and benefits advisor. Your staff of assistants works closely with you to advise and help you in carrying out your duties. It is your section's responsibility to:

1. Provide counsel and assistance to all headquarters-building employees, annuitants, and beneficiaries in matters relating to participation in company benefit plans.
2. Counsel with and assist supervisors and employee-relations staffs concerning administrative procedures related to benefit plans.
3. Advise employee relations and other staffs concerning the implications of proposed changes in the benefit plans for procedures and current practices and vice versa.
4. Advise all staff members of the content of employee communications.

You and each of your colleagues have a number of staff assistants working for you. One of them is to be promoted to fill a vacancy as a compensation and benefits advisor. You have individually looked over your staff, and each of you has selected the one that you consider to be the best qualified to get the promotion. You are meeting today to decide which person should be promoted.

Here is your time schedule:

1. You have fifteen minutes to read the description of your candidate and prepare a five-minute oral presentation of your candidate for the job.
2. Organize your presentation to present as accurate and convincing a description of your candidate as possible. Your associates should be made to realize that you know this person well and to understand why you believe he or she is well qualified for this promotion. The oral presentations will take twenty minutes.
3. After the presentations, group members are to spend the next thirty minutes discussing the qualifications of each candidate with the presenters, doing the best they can for their candidates. At the end of the discussion, the group selects the candidate most qualified.

Because there will be other openings, the group is to rank the other candidates according to who will be promoted second, third, and fourth. Remember, presenters, it will be to your advantage to get your candidate selected. Morale will improve in your own area and your chances will increase for functioning effectively with the new compensation and benefits advisor.

4. The presenters take five minutes to complete the Self-Evaluation forms.
5. The group has twenty minutes for the observers to give feedback to the presenters, who then compare these recommendations to those they made for themselves on the Self-Evaluation form.

PRESENTATION EVALUATION

1. What did each presenter do best during the presentation? (Think in terms of organization, logic, humor, persuasiveness, body language, tone of voice, poise, confidence, etc.)

Presenter 1 (Bill Johnson):

Presenter 2 (Susan Jones):

Presenter 3 (Roberta Smith):

Presenter 4 (John Taylor):

2. List three aspects of the presentation for each person that could be changed or improved.

Presenter 1 (Bill Johnson):

Presenter 2 (Susan Jones):

Presenter 3 (Roberta Smith):

Presenter 4 (John Taylor):

SELF-EVALUATION

1. What do you think you did best during your presentation? (Think of tone of voice, body language, use of logic, persuasiveness, etc.)

2. List three aspects of your presentation that you would like to change and/or improve. How specifically would you like to change them?

36 Career Planning for Women

Purposes

I. To gain a clear sense of direction in developing one's own career plan.

II. To identify short-term and long-range goals in career development.

III. To make action plans for goal achievement.

Group Size

Since this procedure requires personal counseling and review at each stage, the facilitator should work with a small group of not more than twelve people.

Time Required

Four two-hour sessions scheduled one week apart.

Setting

This career-development procedure is designed to extend over a period of one month, with weekly two-hour sessions for guidance. It can be conducted either as a public offering or as an in-house organizational program for women. The participants should be prepared to do some of the work between sessions.

Materials

I. A copy of the Self-Analysis Questionnaire and a pencil for each participant.

II. Each participant should have access to (at home or in a nearby library) a large (metropolitan-area) Telephone Directory Yellow Pages.

III. A copy of Career Investigation for each participant.

IV. A copy of Development Plan for each participant.

Procedure

SESSION 1:

I. It is assumed that the participants understand that they are here to engage in a career-planning process. Open the first session by presenting the following overview of what the process will be like:

The materials for this procedure were furnished by Elizabeth Wales, Ph.D., Department of Psychiatry, Wright State University School of Medicine, Dayton, Ohio.

Schedule

Session 1: Self-analysis
Session 2: Identifying areas of interest
Session 3: Career investigation
Session 4: Goal setting and action planning

Take appropriate climate-building steps to get the participants introduced to one another. They should be prepared for an open sharing of personal hopes and doubts during the course of the four sessions.

II. Hand out a copy of the Self-Analysis Questionnaire and a pencil to each of the participants, announcing the following:

You have about an hour to work through this questionnaire. It should be done with careful thought and attention, and you should answer the questions as honestly as possible. At a certain time (forty-five minutes before the end of the session) you will be asked to give a two-minute presentation, as described on the first page of the questionnaire.

III. As the group members work through the questionnaire, you should remain constantly available to encourage, answer questions, review work in progress, and keep motivation high.

IV. At the time announced, assemble the group and hear the two-minute presentations. It is usually best to keep intervening comments to a minimum until all have been heard; then conduct an open discussion on:

A. What did you learn about yourself from this activity?
B. What did you learn from the others in this process?

V. Give the assignment for the second session as follows:

A. Using a large metropolitan area Telephone Directory Yellow Pages, go through and mark with a star *any* entry that arouses an interest in you for any reason. This will take several hours, and probably several sittings, to complete.

B. Bring to the next session the list of entries that you starred. Also bring back the questionnaire we completed in this session.

SESSION 2:

I. Hand out pencils to each of the members and ask them to work in pairs as follows:

A. Review your list with your partner and categorize the items. You had some reason for checking the items that you did. The reasons may not be evident in just the names of the entries. Talk about why you checked these items. Go back to your questionnaire, particularly Part II, and see if that may help you to identify categories.

B. Your task is to work both with your partner and alone to find four or five major categories of interest and to list the items under these categories so that they become sorted out. If you have time, try to name specific jobs in each category that you would like to do.

II. Allow about thirty minutes for this task. Then ask for a report from each participant. The facilitator and the group serve as consultants as the reports are made, with the possibility of sharpening the categories or adding to them. (About one hour.)

III. Hand out the Career Investigation forms to each participant and assign the following task to be done before the third session:

> The task is for each of you to meet with people in two or three areas of your interest, as derived from your categories, to learn as much as you can about a job or position. Use part 2 of the Career Investigation forms to guide you in your interview. Be prepared to report at the third session on the interviews you have conducted.

IV. Use the time remaining for the second session to assist each participant to:
1. Identify specific jobs in their areas of interest that they want to inquire about.
2. Identify whom they want to interview by calling on the resources of other group members, the facilitator, or work colleagues and home acquaintances.

SESSION 3:

I. This session is used to take stock and to build self-esteem. There is less busy work than in the other sessions, and, at this point, it is important to provide time for an expression of the hopes and fears of the members. The following is a recommended procedure.

A. Hear reports from each member and discuss the results.
B. Perform a "strength bombardment" for each person, or at least for those most in need of a more positive self-image. Explain the strength bombardment as follows:
   1. A member sits in a chair in the center of the group circle.
   2. The other members bombard the subject with positive comments about any attributes, characteristics, or behaviors they have noted.
   3. The subject listens without comment until the members are finished.
   4. Then the subject responds with any thought or feeling that occurs at that moment.
   5. Using that comment as a cue, the members resume the bombardment for a short time.
   6. The subject returns to the group circle.
C. Conduct a discussion of "your optimism and pessimism regarding the planning of your future."
   Note: Research shows that persons who do not vote in national elections share one thing in common — they do not feel that anything they can do will influence the future. Persons who are suffering depression also feel helpless and see no brightness in the future. On the other hand, persons who have reached their elderly years in good health generally feel optimistic about their own futures.
D. Some members may have scheduled additional interviews for career investigations during the next week. Try to assist them by using the collective experience of the group. Role playing may be appropriate.
E. Announce that the members will engage in a planning activity during the fourth session.

SESSION 4:

I. Hand out a copy of the Development Plan and a pencil to each participant.
II. Assist the members to work through this plan, preferably doing it all together and discussing the various items as they move along. After item 7, which lists activities, it

may be useful for each member to select the activity of top priority and do a force-field analysis (Lewin, 1969; Spier, 1973) to identify the forces that may help or hinder their actually doing the activity.

III. At the conclusion of the fourth session, each participant should have a clear idea of a goal she wants to work toward and of the steps she will take during the next year to meet that goal.

References

Lewin, K. Quasi-stationary social equilibria and the problem of permanent changes. In W. G. Bennis, K. D. Benne, & R. Chin (Eds.), *The planning of change.* New York: Holt, Rinehart, and Winston, 1969.

Spier, M.S. Kurt Lewin's "force-field analysis." In J. E. Jones & J. W. Pfeiffer (Eds.), *The 1973 annual handbook for group facilitators.* San Diego, CA: University Associates, 1973.

SELF-ANALYSIS QUESTIONNAIRE

Instructions:

1. Complete Parts 1 and 2 of this questionnaire as carefully and as honestly as possible.
2. Choose a job that you would like to have in the future. Prepare a two-minute presentation designed to convince the class that you should get the job. Be sure to cover the following three points during your presentation:
   - Job Title
   - Job description — the specific duties and responsibilities.
   - Why you should be hired for this job.

SELF-ANALYSIS QUESTIONNAIRE: PART 1-A

Instructions: Think carefully about all the things you have done in your life. List the five activities you **enjoyed most**. Next to each one, explain **why** these experiences gave you pleasure. Do not limit yourself to work activities.

ACTION **REASON**

SELF-ANALYSIS QUESTIONNAIRE: PART 1-B

Instructions: Think carefully about all of the things you have done in your life. List the five activities you enjoyed **least**. Next to each, explain **why** you did not enjoy these activities. Do not limit yourself to work activities.

ACTION   **REASON**

SELF-ANALYSIS QUESTIONNAIRE: PART 1-C

Instructions: Think carefully about all of the things you have **achieved** in your life. List the five achievements of which you are most **proud**. Next to each achievement, explain **why** you are most proud of this achievement.

ACHIEVEMENT   **REASON**

SELF-ANALYSIS QUESTIONNAIRE: PART 1-D

Instructions: Think carefully about all of the activities you have participated in during your life. List the five situations in which you have felt most confused, frustrated, or otherwise dissatisfied with the results of your efforts. Next to each situation, explain what made you feel as you did.

ACTIVITY   **REASON**

SELF-ANALYSIS QUESTIONNAIRE: PART 2

1. How intelligent am I?

2. When people praise me on the job, what kinds of things do they mention? (Responsibility, neatness, speed, accuracy, mental quickness, etc.)

3. Do I have any unusual talent, skills, or knowledge? What kind of activity do I do better than most people? (Write, organize, manage, solve problems, staff work, etc.)

4. What talent or skills do I have today that I did not have one year ago?

5. What talents or resources do I have that are now underutilized and not in the process of being developed?

6. What talents or skills would I like to develop further?

7. Am I satisfied with my career progress to date? Yes _____ No _____ If yes, state reasons. If no, state reasons and list two or three things that may have interfered with advancement.

8. Is my current position bringing me a feeling of accomplishment and satisfaction? Yes _____ No _____ If yes, list parts of the job that give a feeling of accomplishment. If not, list what is missing.

9. Am I considered to be — in the estimation of my peers, my manager and myself — an outstanding performer in my present job? If not, how can I accomplish this?

10. What are the aspects of jobs I have observed or performed that I . . .
    Least Like:

    Most Like:

11. It is often difficult to specify the type of job you would like most. Instead, think of the kinds of things you would like to do in a job. Check the ones that you feel must be in a job you would like:
    _____ a. Calculate, work with figures, keep records
    _____ b. Write, read, research
    _____ c. Invent, imagine, create
    _____ d. Help people, be of service
    _____ e. Organize, systematize, revise
    _____ f. Talk, teach, give speeches
    _____ g. Work independently, own or collect things
    _____ h. Persuade, sell, influence others
    _____ i. Travel, meet with people
    _____ j. Instruct others, supervise, direct
    _____ k. Hand skills, operate a machine, assemble and fix things
    _____ l. Observe, inspect, review work of others
    _____ m. Design color, shape things
    _____ n. Other: _____

12. Do I want to advance or better myself or accept more responsibility?
    Why?

    Why not?

166 *Activities for Trainers: 50 Useful Designs*

CAREER INVESTIGATION: PART 1

Instructions: If you are not absolutely certain about your long- and short-term goals, conduct a career investigation by doing the following:

1. List several general areas of interest that you could **explore** in order to pinpoint specific jobs within the area that is suited to your needs and abilities. (Accounting, sales, programming, production, personnel, etc.)

2. Use the Career Investigation: Part 2 form to explore each of these areas. Arrange to interview a person who is in the field, who knows the field, or who may be hiring in the field. Set up a luncheon meeting or an hour-long appointment with a person in each area you have just listed in order to learn as much as possible about each position. Remember, you are not applying for a job, you are only getting acquainted with what that type of work holds for you.

Part 5. Women's Issues   167

CAREER INVESTIGATION: PART 2

General Area:

Specific Job:

1. What are the specific duties and responsibilities of this job? What does one do all day in this position?

2. What does the person who is presently in the job like or dislike about it?

3. How does this position develop one for future advancement? Where could it lead?

4. What factors or characteristics would make one fail or succeed in this position?

5. What kind of ability, experience, and training is necessary in order to obtain this position?

6. What personal commitments such as overtime or travel are required in order to be successful in this position?

DEVELOPMENT PLAN

1. Based on the analysis of my abilities and needs, I would like my next two positions to be the following:

2. In order to compete successfully for this next position, what knowledge or skill do I need to develop?

        Knowledge   Skill

  a.

  b.

  c.

  d.

  e.

3. What added or new job experiences do I need?

4. What is there in my current job, or what can be added to my current job, to help me get the experience and development I need?

5. Are my goals and values compatible with the policies and opportunities of my present company? Should and would I be willing to change?

6. How can I acquire the necessary training I need?

   a. Company-based programs:

   b. Formal education (high school, college, graduate programs, specialized courses):

   c. Self-development

      Professional periodicals:

      Newspapers:

      Clubs, organizations:

      Books:

7. The following is my personal development plan for the next twelve months:

    Activity   Target Date

8. Long-range goal — I think the highest position I could ever fill would be at the level of:

How do I plan to get there? (What interim jobs are needed?)

How long will it take?

What feedback can I obtain along the way in order to determine whether my plan is working?

Part six
Supervisory Training

37 Supervisory Training: A Workshop Opener

Purposes

I. To start a workshop with an interesting task that involves all participants.
II. To assist participants in getting acquainted with one another.
III. To compare the characteristics of participants who are supervisors with the national norms of supervisors' characteristics.

Group Size

The participants work in small groups of five or six persons each.

Time Required

From one hour to one and one-quarter hours.

Setting

This activity is intended for use at the beginning of a two- or three-day program of supervisory training. Such programs typically have from twenty to thirty participants, and there is a need for a nonthreatening activity to establish a learning climate and to help the members find out something about their fellow participants. The activity achieves these aims, with the further benefit of offering information concerning the role of the supervisor.

Materials

I. A blank flipchart and markers.
II. A copy of the Instructor's Guide for the facilitator.
III. A copy of The Job of the Supervisor for each participant.

Procedure

I. Immediately after opening the session (which may include your self-introduction as the facilitator and announcements of necessary housekeeping details such as time schedules, breaks, etc.), indicate that a common interest among supervisors is: How do we compare with other supervisors? Announce that some answers will be provided in this activity. Outline on the flipchart the following procedure:
   A. The participants form small groups of five or six persons, preferably strangers to one another.
   B. The facilitator provides a series of questions for the groups to discuss.
   C. The groups report on the answers and averages produced by their discussions.
   D. The facilitator reports on results of national surveys of supervisors so that the supervisors in this group can compare themselves with the national averages.

II. Follow the procedure:
   A. Help the members to form small groups.
   B. Ask the following questions one at a time, allowing sufficient time for discussion of each:
      1. How many people do you supervise?
      2. What is your average age?
      3. With whom do you spend your time?
      4. Can supervisors join unions?
      5. Do you do the same work as the people you supervise?
      6. What are your most pressing problems?
      7. How do you learn to do your job better?
      8. Why do supervisors fail?
   C.-D. The periods of reporting from the groups and comparing group results with the survey results may be used for further discussion of the topics and for increasing acquaintanceship among the members. For instance, who supervises the most people, etc. Use the Instructor's Guide for reporting the national survey results.
III. After the last question has been discussed, hand out a copy of The Job of the Supervisor to each participant.
   A. This list may be used simply as a summary of the previous discussion or as something the participants put in their take-home packet.
   B. The hand-out may be put to a more complete use by asking the small groups to go through the list and identify the items they definitely include among their responsibilities and those that do not fit their organizational settings. A final report from the small groups on this question will help to describe the job of supervisor as seen by this particular group.

THE JOB OF THE SUPERVISOR

1. Establish the climate of human relationships at the departmental level.
2. Shape the attitudes that motivate employees toward better performance.
3. Interpret and apply policies, work specifications, and job orders.
4. Train new employees and instruct older employees to work effectively and safely.
5. Counsel and discipline employees.
6. Initiate or recommend personnel actions such as promotions, transfers, pay increases, and discharges.
7. Plan and maintain time and work schedules.
8. Adjust and improve work procedures, using knowledge of machine and equipment capacities.
9. Take necessary steps to secure the good quality of products and services for which the supervisor is responsible.
10. Coordinate the activities of the department in such a way that its goals are met economically.

Note: The word **supervisor** derives from **superior** and **overseer**. At one time, it meant **master**. Other titles used today include **front-line supervisor, foreman, first-line supervisor, section manager,** or **department head**.

Reprinted from pp. 3-4 of **What Every Supervisor Should Know** (3rd ed.) by Lester R. Bittle. Copyright © 1974 by McGraw-Hill, Inc. Used with the permission of McGraw-Hill Book Company.

INSTRUCTOR'S GUIDE

1. How many people do you supervise?

    This depends on the type of operations performed. If there is a single operation with high employee density, perhaps fifty workers can be supervised by one person. With dispersed operations, or where the supervisor must keep in close touch with every operation (such as in a flight-control tower), the number may go down to five or be in the range of ten to twenty.

2. What is your average age?
    - First supervisory assignments come, on the average, at about the age of 33.
    - About 12 percent of all supervisors are between twenty and thirty years of age.
    - The average age of supervisors is about forty-two years.

3. With whom do you spend your time?

	Percent of Time
Alone	33
With own employees	30
With other supervisors	8
With superiors	7
With maintenance and service personnel	6
With others	16

    As a rule, corrective measures should be taken to raise the time with employees to 50 percent.

4. Can supervisors join unions?
    - The Taft-Hartley Act places supervisors as part of the management group and as such they are excluded from union membership.
    - About one percent of all supervisors belong to a supervisors' union, but they are not encouraged to bargain collectively.
    - Supervisors' unions are denied protection under the National Labor Relations Board.
    - Surveys of supervisors, even those who had formerly been union members, found that 75 percent said they should stay out of unions because they "can't serve two masters."

5. Do you do the same work as the people you supervise?

    There is no law to stop it, but unions frown on it except in emergencies. Management usually agrees. Organizations want you to supervise the work of others, not do it for them. It makes little sense for a higher salaried person to perform lower paid work.

6. What are your most pressing problems?
    - Meeting tight production schedules. The job is still one of getting out the production.
    - Keeping production up to standard, keeping efficient, and keeping costs down.
    - Maintaining cooperative attitudes with employees.

    Other problems:
    - Motivating people to do good work.
    - Maintaining a neat and orderly workplace — housekeeping.
    - Controlling waste.
    - Maintaining equipment.
    - Employee training.

The data for the answers to the questions posed in this activity were obtained from **What Every Supervisor Should Know** (3rd ed.) by Lester R. Bittle. Copyright © 1974 by McGraw-Hill, Inc. Used with the permission of McGraw-Hill Book Company.

7. How do you learn to do your job better?
    - "Learning is caught, not taught."
    - Few people have time to stop to teach you.
    - Be awake, observant, and eager to learn, and you will learn.
    - Take your own responsibility to do things better.
    - When you see someone you respect do something you do not understand, ask why.
    - If something does not work out, you may ask your boss for suggestions.
8. Why do supervisors fail?
    - Poor personal relations with workers or with other management people.
    - Individual shortcomings, such as lack of initiative, emotional instability.
    - Lack of understanding of the management point of view.
    - Unwillingness to spend the necessary time and effort to improve.
    - Inability to adjust to new and changing conditions.

38 Supervisory Training: Role Clarification

Purposes

I. To identify uncertainties in the limits of a supervisor's authority.

II. To examine peripheral elements that typically lead to role conflict.

III. To plan for increased role clarification.

Group Size

The participants work in small groups of five or six persons each.

Time Required

One hour.

Setting

This activity is appropriate for use in a supervisory training program. The instrument, Boundary Limits of Your Position, is also useful for any group of employees, including managers, for purposes of team building.

Materials

I. A copy of Authority Limits of Supervisory Positions and a pencil for each participant.

II. A copy of Boundary Limits of Your Position for each participant.

Procedure

I. Present an introduction to *role theory* that covers the following points:

A. Your job description defines a role you must play to meet the objectives of your unit.

B. You also bring your personal style to this job — your personality and behavior help to define your role.

C. Your role is also made up of what others expect of you, i.e., your subordinates, your boss, the union, visitors, other supervisors, etc. They may expect different things of you and these expectations give you problems on occasion.

D. Another complicating factor is that each of us has several roles to take at the same time. Not only do we have the role attached to our position at work but also roles as, perhaps, a parent, a spouse, a good friend, a student, and as a leader in our club, church, or community. Usually, one role is dominant in any situation, and it is easy to use the appropriate behaviors for it. Sometimes, however, roles conflict. For instance, when your spouse calls you at work to make demands on your time and attention, you may feel torn between conflicting pressures. Role conflict comes when simultaneous and incompatible expectations are imposed on you.

E. Conflict on the job often results from conflicting role expectations related to how much authority you have and to ambiguities around role boundaries or the peripheral elements of the job. We are going to use some questionnaires to help examine these.

II. Divide the participants into groups and hand out Authority Limits for Supervisory Positions and a pencil to each person.

A. Instruct the participants to use the guide at the top of the questionnaire and mark a 1, 2, or 3 after each item to indicate how much authority they believe they have.

B. Ask the group members to compare their responses with one another, looking for differences in how they rated each item. Are the differences due to their own attitudes or to directives they have received? On which items are they unsure?

III. Allow about twenty minutes and then get a report from each group asking:

A. On what items were different ratings found?

B. What were the reasons given?

C. What other responsibility areas not mentioned on the questionnaire give you trouble because you are uncertain of the extent of your authority?

IV. Hand out Boundary Limits of Your Position and instruct groups as follows:

A. Imagine that you are preparing to discuss your job or position with your superior. On this form make notes of items that you particularly want to clarify. (Five minutes.)

B. Now that you have made your notes, select those areas most important to yourselves and discuss with your team how you can work with your superior to achieve a clearer understanding of these areas.

V. Near the end of the hour, ask each group to share briefly some of the content of its discussion. Then, summarize with the following points:

A. When role conflict occurs, it is apt to have consequences such as reducing your effectiveness or satisfaction with your work. In the extreme, it can produce anxiety or drive people from their jobs.

B. Role conflict can be reduced by:

1. Ranking your role obligations in priority according to power. For instance, you will fulfill your superior's expectations before those of your subordinates; or, an emergency call from your family will always take precedence over work demands.

2. Separate your roles physically; decide that the job and home are going to be separate. In each place be fully occupied with the most appropriate role behaviors of that place. A consequence of this, for instance, will be a reduction of taking your work home.

3. Clarify ambiguities by talking them over with your supervisor. Both you and the supervisor will be better able to function with a clear understanding on these issues.

4. Continue to work on your own development. Examine your personal strengths and weaknesses. What educational needs can be met, or what personal characteristics do you need to work on?

BOUNDARY LIMITS OF YOUR POSITION

Instructions: Most people have a clear idea of the requirements and expectations of the key elements of their positions. However, confusion often exists on the peripheral elements. One way to clarify roles is to negotiate understandings with your superior on areas of uncertainty.

Consider your job in relation to each of the following items. Make notes of any areas in which you are uncertain. Your notes should be specific enough (people, incidents, conditions, times, places) to prepare you for discussing the matter with your supervisor for clarification. What solution would you recommend to your supervisor?

1. **Work Flow:** Who has to do his or her job before you can do yours? Who cannot do his or her job until you do yours? Identify the several boundaries of your position.

2. **Resources:** What must happen, or what resources must be available, before you can do your job?

3. **Decision Making:** In what areas can you make decisions without checking with your boss? Where are you uncertain about your authority?

4. **Overlapping**: Where does your area of responsibility border on someone else's? How can you be clear on who does what?

5. **Gaps and Initiative**: Should you take responsibility in an area that is not being covered or does your supervisor just want you to call attention to their existence?

6. **Line of Authority**: Is there a clear and agreed-upon chain of responsibility? Do you know to whom you are responsible?

7. **Multiple Bosses**: Are there some situations in which you must report to and meet the expectations of several persons?

8. **Interpersonal Relations**: Is there any uncertainty regarding who is a:
    - Subordinate (you can control)?
    - Peer (you must work **with**)?
    - Superior (you cannot control)?

AUTHORITY LIMITS OF SUPERVISORY POSITIONS

Instructions: As a supervisor, you and your immediate superior should be in agreement on how much authority you have. Three levels of authority are described under "Authority Limits." Using this three-point scale, read the functions listed below and rank each according to the limits of your authority in performing that function.

Authority Limits:

1. Complete authority: supervisor can take action without consulting with superior.
2. Limited authority: to the extent that supervisor **must inform** superior of any action taken.
3. Very limited authority: in that supervisor **must consult** with superior before taking any action.

New Employees:
    Hire additional employees　　_____
    Accept new employees　　_____
    Report on probationary employees　　_____

Job Assignments:
    Schedule employees　　_____
    Make changes in schedules　　_____
    Transfer employees within department　　_____
    Transfer employees to another department　　_____

Discipline:
    Suggest appropriate discipline　　_____
    Issue written reprimand　　_____
    Suspend　　_____
    Discharge for cause　　_____

Grievances:
    Adjust grievances with employees　　_____
    Accept written grievances from union　　_____
    Give written reply to union　　_____

Termination and Leaves:
    Grant leaves of absence　　_____
    Prepare vacation schedules　　_____
    Lay employees off for lack of work　　_____

Information:
    Maintain bulletin boards　　_____
    Explain policy to employees　　_____

First Aid and Accidents:
    Send employees to first-aid station　　_____
    Send employees to doctor or hospital　　_____
    Notify family of injured employee　　_____
    Prepare report of accident　　_____

Safety and Good Housekeeping:
    Take unsafe tools out of service　　_____
    Correct unsafe conditions　　_____
    Stop work where conditions are unsafe　　_____
    Establish housekeeping standards　　_____

39 House of Cards

Purposes

I. To form an organization that produces a product.

II. To examine the group and intergroup dynamics that came into play in the organization.

III. To increase one's understanding of these dynamics in one's own organization.

Group Size

The participants are divided into several small groups of five to seven persons each.

Time Required

One and one-half hours.

Setting

This activity has been used in training supervisors. It helps them to take a larger view of their organization than they usually do from within their own subunit. It can also be used in training managers and students as an introduction to the dimensions of an organization that come under scrutiny in an organization development program. A large room is required with teams seated around tables.

Materials

I. A pack of fifty index cards per group.

II. A supply of the following materials for each group:
- A five-foot length of masking tape
- Two markers or crayons: one red and one green
- Thirty paper clips

III. A copy of the Judges' Rating Form and a pencil for each group.

IV. Paper and a pencil for each participant.

V. A blank flipchart and markers.

Procedure

I. Collect a few coins from each participant by passing a hat or box, explaining that the combined contributions will constitute the prize to the winning team.

II. State the purpose of the organization, as described previously under Purposes.

III. Assign the initial task to the teams (groups already seated at tables) and postpone answering any questions about what the job will be:

> You have ten minutes to talk about how you want to organize yourselves to perform the job that I am going to give you.

Part 6. Supervisory Training

IV. After ten minutes, give each group its materials and an identifying number or name.
V. Reveal the following task, which has already been printed on the flipchart:

>Construct a structure that will be best in terms of
>1. Creative use of the materials
>2. Aesthetic values
>
>You will have forty minutes for this task.

VI. After about thirty minutes of action, select a person from each team and meet with these people off to one side. Tell them that they are to change their roles at this point and become judges. Give them each a copy of the Judges' Rating Form and instruct them in its use. Tell them they will have about ten minutes to visit each group and to make their ratings.
VII. After ten minutes, collect the rating forms from all the judges and calculate the average rating for each group. The winning team is the group with the highest average rating.
VIII. Announce the winning team and award the cash prize. Allow the judges to return to their teams.
IX. Interview the judges briefly about the conflicts they experienced. This is not important to the overall task, but it helps to extend appreciation to them and to make them feel OK.
X. Provide a brief overview of the organizational dynamics that probably came into play as the teams worked together. Include the following, writing the words on the flipchart to guide the subsequent discussion:

Leadership	Decision making	Competition
Division of labor	Followership	Conflicts due to loyalty
Delegation	Rewards	Morale

XI. Ask the groups to discuss these elements as they experienced them during the activity.
XII. After ten minutes, ask for reports from the groups. One way of having groups report is to ask Team A to report on its leadership, Team B to report on its decision-making process, etc.
XIII. Hand out paper and pencil to each participant and suggest:

>Jot down notes as reminders to yourselves about these questions: How was my behavior typical of me, and how would I behave differently in order to be more effective in a group?

XIV. Summarize by stating:

>Every group that joins together to do work becomes an organization. The organizational dynamics at work in this activity are similar to those of much larger organizations such as those you work in back home. The pressures you may have felt here are also on your bosses and supervisors. An organization that wants to improve itself looks at dimensions such as these, which may be more important than such individual aspects as personality.

JUDGES' RATING FORM

Instructions: Your task is to rate the structure of each group. Please give a grade to each structure, from 1 to 100, just as a professor might grade a test. A grade of below 70 would be very poor, a grade in the 80s is average, and a grade in the 90s is excellent. A grade in the high 90s will be rare.

Use the following two criteria for your decisions:

A. Creative use of the materials.
   Does the structure show that the group went beyond building a simple "house of cards?"
B. Aesthetic values.
   Does the structure achieve a sense of beauty and harmony that is pleasing to look at?

Record your judgments below and return this sheet to the facilitator within the next ten minutes.

GROUP	GRADE
1.	_____
2.	_____
3.	_____
4.	_____
5.	_____
6.	_____

40 Giving Orders

Purposes

I. To identify a scale of order giving, representing styles from tentative to severe.

II. To practice the skill of selecting and using different styles of giving orders.

III. To compare one's own style of giving orders with others'.

Group Size

From fifteen to twenty-five persons who work individually and in small groups.

Time Required

One and one-half hours.

Setting

This activity can be used for management training, supervisory training, or for any group that wishes to focus on the interpersonal relations between a superior and a subordinate in a work setting.

Materials

I. A copy of The Case of the Meeting Room and a pencil for each participant.

Procedure

I. Introduce the activity by asking:

When giving orders, have you experienced difficulty in finding the right words in order to get work done and at the same time maintain the optimum relationship with your employees? What are the settings in which you provide direct supervision of the work of others?

II. Indicate that there are several kinds of orders that can be placed on a scale from tentative to severe. Each type has different consequences. Display the following scale on a flipchart:

A SCALE OF ORDERS

Type	Consequence
1. Suggest	Tentative. You are open to alternatives.
2. Request	Gives a feeling of freedom.
3. Instruct and require	Gives a feeling of being closely supervised. Sometimes builds resentment.
4. Order or command	Often causes resentment and resistance. To be used in emergencies.

III. Divide the participants into groups of five or six persons. Give each person a pencil and a copy of The Case of the Meeting Room and announce the following instructions:

    A. Write a complete answer to each situation in the very words you would use.

    B. Following your completion of the case, discuss and compare the answers you have given to each question with the members of your group. Each group is to decide the best answer for that situation, considering the consequences. You will have a total of forty-five minutes to accomplish this.

IV. At the end of the small-group discussion, leave the groups where they are and ask each group to take a turn and give its answer to one of the questions (1 through 8 in the case). Each group will be expected to defend its answer by responding to questions posed by members of the other groups. As the groups present their answers, indicate on the flipchart where the answers fall on A Scale of Orders.

V. Conclude the session by asking for quick responses to the following questions:

1. Should you repeat an order?
2. Can you be at fault when an employee misses an order?
3. What should you do when an employee willfully refuses to do what you tell him (or her)?
4. Should you ever communicate an order in writing? if so, when?
5. Can you let an employee use his or her own judgment on whether to follow instructions?
6. Should you let anyone else give instructions to your employees?
7. Can you give orders to a group and have them be effective?

THE CASE OF THE MEETING ROOM

Instructions: Your boss has asked you to get a large room ready for an important meeting. The meeting will occur tomorrow and last all day. Some important speakers will address about thirty people. Outside guests will be attending and you want the place to be comfortable and look attractive. Although this is not in your regular line of duty, you have agreed to see to it, and you want to do a good job. You have asked two people to be here this morning to help you. One of them, Mary, is with you. She is a young colleague, new to her job. John has not shown up yet. He is a helper in the office cafeteria and you have the dietitian's permission to use him for a couple of hours.

The room is rarely used but it is in an upstairs corner of your building and has excellent potential. It is carpeted and has draperied windows and a good view. Someone has stored some heavy cartons and about sixty chairs there. You envision the setting that you need as an audience-style setup of chairs facing the speakers, a podium, a flipchart, and a small table.

1. You have a fair idea of how you want to arrange the room. What do you tell Mary? Write down exactly what you would say, in one sentence.

2. You decide first to clear the area for the podium and table. You want Mary to help you move the heavy podium. What do you say to her?

3. After you have been working at dusting things off for about thirty minutes, John shows up. Work has been difficult because the room is crowded with the boxes and excess chairs. What do you say to John?

4. In order to get the excess chairs stored in the next room, what do you say to John?

190   Activities for Trainers: 50 Useful Designs

5. The room is beginning to take shape, but the carpet needs to be vacuumed. The vacuum cleaners are two floors down (no elevators) in a maintenance storage room. You also need window-cleaning fluid and paper towels for cleaning the windows. What do you say to get these things?

6. Mary offers to vacuum the rug, and you and John start on the windows. He notices that a drapery has come unattached at one corner of the window he is working on, so that it sags from the rod. You noticed it too, but have not had time to think much about it. John has pulled a small table over to the window and is putting a chair on it to reach the top of the drapery. You are suddenly concerned that he will fall. A ladder is needed. What do you say?

7. Suppose he insists the he will be all right. What do you say?

8. Finally the room looks as it should. You sit down in one of the chairs to rest a bit. Then you notice that you have arranged the room backwards. The audience is facing the windows. The speaker will be a silhouette and the audience will suffer eyestrain. All the chairs must be turned around, the podium moved, etc. What do you say?

Part seven
The Training of Consultants

41 Consultant's Check List for Initial Client Contact

The role of a consultant for training or organizational change is neither that of a salesman nor of a therapist. It falls somewhere in between. If the initial contact with a client is successful, a consultant will be chosen in preference to possible competitors and will expect payment for services, and these services will require the development of a close interpersonal relationship. The consultant must make a favorable professional impression, but the service provided will not usually be directed toward any personality change in the client.

The following brief check list can be used as a reminder by consultants before they conduct an interview with a client; it also provides an introduction to the teaching of consultation skills. You may want to make notes for each item about yourself, about what you typically do, or fail to do, or want to learn to do.

1. Discover what the dimensions of the problem are, from the client's point of view. Goals can only be set as you gain clarity in identifying the problem.
2. Search for the client's motives in developing a program. As a means of building a bridge between the two of you, find areas in which the client's goals and your goals are similar.
3. Test the extent to which the client can become involved by inquiring into the client's willingness to take risks (financial, structural, personnel assignments) in order to accomplish something real.
4. Talk the client's language. Prepare yourself ahead of time to show that you know something about the environment in which the client works.
5. Confront the client on important issues directly enough to make the contact memorable. Ask a crucial question or two. Question some basic or hidden assumptions.
6. Demonstrate that you can be influenced by the client. Show flexibility in dealing with realities such as time, setting, limitations, and reasonable expectations.
7. Bring the client as a *person* to the transaction, not just in the official role. Obtain information concerning the client's position in the organization, doubts or self-assurance about competence, and his or her needs.
8. Indicate clearly the degree to which you think success is possible, either from your own previous experience or that of your colleagues.
9. Ask what questions the client may have about you that have not yet been asked.
10. Establish a psychological contract with the client. What do you expect from the client and what can be expected from you? Start by being very clear about the time and form of the immediate next steps.

42 Consultant Skills: Interviewing

Purposes

I. To compare a self-assessment of interviewing skills with an assessment by another person, after observation.

II. To identify the attitudes and behaviors of a consultant that need improvement in conducting an interview.

Group Size

Participants work in trios. The total group can be of any reasonable size, such as a training conference or workshop.

Time Required

A minimum of two hours, preferably a half-day or three to three and one-half hours.

Setting

A room large enough to seat all participants for an instruction period. After that, trios are self-directed and can work in any quiet, comfortable setting.

Materials

I. A pencil and a copy of Form A: Self-Assessment Form, Consultant Interviewing Skills for each participant.

II. A copy of Form B: Feedback to Interviewer Form for each participant.

III. A copy of Form C: A Guide to Learning for each participant.

Procedure

I. Explain that this activity offers each participant an opportunity to:

   A. Assess your own skills and behaviors as a consultant who is conducting an interview with a person seeking help.

   B. Practice and demonstrate your interviewing and helping skills by working with a person seeking help.

   C. Receive structured feedback from the interviewee and from an observer, and identify your skill areas that are in need of further development.

II. Divide the group into trios and ask them to be seated again for further instruction. (If the total number of participants does not allow for a final trio, it is better to form a final set of two pairs than to form a quartet.)

III. Hand out copies of Form A and pencils to all participants, announcing that they have ten minutes to complete it. Tell them not to consult with one another while doing this.

IV. Distribute Form B to all participants and explain:

   A. This form has the same content as Form A, except that it is written in the past tense. The members of each trio are to take turns as the interviewer, as the person seeking help, and as the observer.

   B. When you are acting as an observer, you rate the interviewer on Form B and act as timekeeper, stopping the interview at the end of twenty minutes. Take a few minutes to complete Form B, and then you will be able to compare the interviewer's self-assessment, Form A, with the observer's feedback, Form B. Take about fifteen minutes to discuss the behaviors or attitudes you noted and used as the basis of your ratings. The interviewee can also participate in the discussion and serve as a reality check on the assumptions and interpretations made by the observer.

   C. In the "Discrepancy Score" column of Form A, you can note the numerical difference between the ratings on Form A and Form B. Those items with the largest difference may be a good place to start your discussion.

V. On a flipchart, display the following suggested time sequence:

TIME SCHEDULE

Member 1 interviews Member 2 while Member 3 observes.	20 minutes
Member 3 completes Form B on Member 1 (the interviewer)	5 minutes
Trio discusses the interview	15 minutes
Member 3 interviews Member 1 while Member 2 observes.	20 minutes
Member 2 completes Form B on Member 3 (the interviewer).	5 minutes
Trio discusses the interview	15 minutes
The three members shift roles and repeat the procedure once again.	40 minutes

VI. Suggest the following criteria to aid the participants in selecting a problem:

   A. It should be a real problem, not fiction — a problem of real concern to you and one for which you do not presently see a solution.

   B. You should be central to the issue; it is your problem and not someone else's. Any solution should depend in part on what you choose to do about it.

   C. A relationship or organizational problem often works best for this activity, but remember that the limited time will not permit an extended recounting of background and historical antecedents.

VII. Distribute Form C to all participants, mentioning that the discussion following each interview is one of the more important opportunities for learning and that this guide may foster the learning process.

VIII. Ask the trios to begin their work.

FORM A: SELF-ASSESSMENT FORM
CONSULTANT INTERVIEWING SKILLS

Your Name _____

Instructions: After each of the following statements, circle a number to represent the manner in which you try to help others and your characteristic behaviors in the consulting role.

	Usually I Do Not				**Usually I Do**	**Discrepancy Score**
1. Give advice	1	2	3	4	5	_____
2. Speak about a client's feelings	1	2	3	4	5	_____
3. Misunderstand what the client says	1	2	3	4	5	_____
4. Approve of the client	1	2	3	4	5	_____
5. Hold myself aloof	1	2	3	4	5	_____
6. Paraphrase client's thoughts and feelings	1	2	3	4	5	_____
7. Enable client to express himself or herself	1	2	3	4	5	_____
8. Avoid giving advice	1	2	3	4	5	_____
9. Seem insensitive to client's feelings	1	2	3	4	5	_____
10. Really listen and remember what client says	1	2	3	4	5	_____
11. See the client as someone he or she is not	1	2	3	4	5	_____
12. Reveal something of myself	1	2	3	4	5	_____
13. Disapprove of client	1	2	3	4	5	_____
14. Help client to see his or her weaknesses	1	2	3	4	5	_____
15. Make it difficult for client to express herself or himself	1	2	3	4	5	_____
16. Solve the problem for the client	1	2	3	4	5	_____
17. Clarify what the client is trying to say	1	2	3	4	5	_____
18. Interrupt client's sentences	1	2	3	4	5	_____

	Usually I Do Not				Usually I Do	Discrepancy Score
19. See the client as an able person	1	2	3	4	5	_____
20. Give new information	1	2	3	4	5	_____
21. Judge the client unfavorably	1	2	3	4	5	_____
22. Protect client from being hurt	1	2	3	4	5	_____
23. Challenge the client	1	2	3	4	5	_____
24. Share my feelings by speaking about them	1	2	3	4	5	_____
25. Feel discomfort with client's uncertainty	1	2	3	4	5	_____
26. Find the real problem	1	2	3	4	5	_____
27. Use platitudes or essentially meaningless phrases	1	2	3	4	5	_____
28. Help client to see his or her own competence	1	2	3	4	5	_____
29. Allow pauses for thought	1	2	3	4	5	_____
30. See the client realistically	1	2	3	4	5	_____
31. Feel uncomfortable	1	2	3	4	5	_____
32. Ask questions that provoke further thought	1	2	3	4	5	_____
33. Present alternatives for the clients to consider	1	2	3	4	5	_____
34. Put into words how the client feels	1	2	3	4	5	_____

FORM B:
FEEDBACK TO INTERVIEWER FORM

Interviewer's Name _____

Instructions: After each of the following statements, circle a number on the scale to represent the manner in which the consultant tried to be helpful and the behaviors characteristic of him or her in the consulting role.

	Not Characteristic				**Characteristic**
1. Gave Advice	1	2	3	4	5
2. Spoke about the client's feelings	1	2	3	4	5
3. Misunderstood what the client said	1	2	3	4	5
4. Approved of the client	1	2	3	4	5
5. Held himself or herself aloof from the client	1	2	3	4	5
6. Paraphrased client's thought and feelings	1	2	3	4	5
7. Enabled client to express himself or herself	1	2	3	4	5
8. Avoided giving advice	1	2	3	4	5
9. Seemed insensitive to client's feelings	1	2	3	4	5
10. Really listened and remembered what client said	1	2	3	4	5
11. Saw the client as someone he or she was not	1	2	3	4	5
12. Revealed something of himself or herself	1	2	3	4	5
13. Disapproved of client	1	2	3	4	5
14. Helped client to see his or her weaknesses	1	2	3	4	5
15. Made it difficult for client to express himself or herself	1	2	3	4	5
16. Solved the problem for the client	1	2	3	4	5

	Not Characteristic				Characteristic
17. Clarified what the client was trying to say	1	2	3	4	5
18. Interrupted client's sentences	1	2	3	4	5
19. Saw the client as an able person	1	2	3	4	5
20. Gave new information	1	2	3	4	5
21. Judged the client unfavorably	1	2	3	4	5
22. Protected client from being hurt	1	2	3	4	5
23. Challenged the client	1	2	3	4	5
24. Shared feelings by speaking of them	1	2	3	4	5
25. Felt discomfort with client's uncertainty	1	2	3	4	5
26. Found the real problem	1	2	3	4	5
27. Used platitudes or essentially meaningless phrases	1	2	3	4	5
28. Helped client to see his or her own competence	1	2	3	4	5
29. Allowed pauses for thought	1	2	3	4	5
30. Saw the client realistically	1	2	3	4	5
31. Felt uncomfortable	1	2	3	4	5
32. Asked questions that provoked further thought	1	2	3	4	5
33. Presented alternatives for the client to consider	1	2	3	4	5
34. Put into words how the client felt	1	2	3	4	5

FORM C:
A GUIDE TO LEARNING

Giving and receiving feedback are additional skills you can practice during this activity. During the discussion period, the focus will be on the attitudes and behavior of the interviewer. Please guard against the temptation to continue with a discussion of the problem that was presented.

To the observer:

- Base your ratings as much as possible on what you see — on observed behavior.
- When you rate an interviewer on the basis of your intuition or feelings, be ready to admit that your data is more subjective.

To the interviewer:

- Listen with an open mind and turn off your defenses for a while.
- See what you can learn from your observer's ratings and comments.
- You do not have to explain yourself. Your job is to **hear** and understand as well as you can.
- Items that have a high discrepancy score indicate areas you may want to explore for further information because your self-assessment on these characteristics differed widely from your observer's ratings.

To the interviewee:

- It is to be hoped that you received some help on your problem, but that is not the main point of this activity. The focus is on the interviewer.
- During the feedback/learning part of the activity you can support or deny the observer's notes according to your feelings and how you experienced the interviewer. Was the interview helpful? If not, why not?

43 Consultation Skills: Planning the Next Visit

Purposes

I. To heighten awareness of the need for planning in consultation.

II. To develop skills in joint planning between consultant and client.

Group Size

From six to twenty-one participants who work in trios.

Time Required

One hour.

Setting

This activity can be used in the training of a variety of persons whose positions call for them to work as outside consultants, such as an organization consultant, a state or county supervisor, a visiting teacher, a mental-health or mental-retardation official, etc. Training programs for persons in such helping roles often emphasize the initial stages of forming a client-consultant relationship. What skills are needed after such a relationship is built? In this activity the focus is on such skills, including the balance of power in deciding on the next step, the need for continuous monitoring of the client's needs, and renegotiation of expectations.

Materials

I. A copy of The Assistant Personnel Director role play for one third of the participants.

II. A copy of The Consultant role play for one third of the participants.

III. A copy of the Observer's Guide *plus* copies of The Assistant Personnel Director and The Consultant role plays for one third of the participants.

IV. A pencil for each participant.

Procedure

I. Explain the purpose and rationale for the activity, including the need for planning each next visit to the client's organization before the end of the current visit. Indicate that this will be done in an interview situation, with an observer helping the role players to learn from the experience.

II. Explain the setting as a large manufacturing plant and the characters as the following:

A. The consultant is a state employee in the department of health. He or she is a specialist in alcoholism. The job requires the consultant to visit industrial settings to elicit the interest of management in setting up a referral system for troubled employees, many of whom are in difficulty because of alcoholism.

Part 7. The Training of Consultants

B. The client is the assistant director of personnel who has been charged with responsibility for the project.

C. The consultant and the client have a twenty-minute interview after which they will have fifteen minutes to discuss it with their observer. The hour will end with a general sharing of learnings.

III. Indicate that the focus of the discussion will be on the following questions:

A. What do you want as a consultant?

B. What does the client want?

C. How did you arrive at the plan for the next visit?

IV. Divide the participants into trios, designating the consultant, client, and observer in each trio. Hand out the respective role-play and observer materials and pencils. Tell the trios they have twenty minutes for the interview and fifteen minutes to discuss the interview with the observer.

V. Announce the twenty-minute and fifteen-minute time limits, then call the trios together to share their observations. The following can be used to guide the discussion:

A. Will trios report the plans they agreed to for the next visit?

B. Will observers report on what learnings were important for them as they watched the process of the interviews?

C. Suppose you consultants were paid by the client rather than being on a state salary. What problems would you have in planning more work? Is this, in part, a conflict of interest?

D. What is your real-life experience in maintaining a continuity of consultation?

THE ASSISTANT PERSONNEL DIRECTOR

Instructions: You are the assistant personnel director in a manufacturing plant that employs about six hundred persons. The personnel director wants to see a program instituted for identification and referral of troubled employees and has delegated you to work with the state consultant and guide this work in the plant.

The purpose of this meeting is to review what has developed so far, and to make plans for the future.

The consultant meets with you during each visit. So far the consultant has held a series of workshops to educate supervisors on how to identify troubled employees and how to use the referral resources in the community. You feel this is a good first step, but time is going by and you are beginning to wonder about the following things:

- What kind of evaluation can be instituted to see whether any real help is being provided to the employees — and to the plant.
- The union is becoming aware of the workshops and you expect that very soon some union leaders will want to become involved so that management will not get all the credit if the program shows success.
- You have become aware that the personnel director's spouse is an incipient alcoholic. What can be done for this special case?

You are torn between two attitudes: (1) you want to show control and direction of the program, but you are uncertain about what you should be aiming for eventually; (2) you want to lead the consultant, but you feel you have to rely on the consultant's expertise for guidance.

At the end of this interview, **you want to make definite plans for what will happen during the next visit of the consultant.**

You have another appointment in about twenty minutes.

THE CONSULTANT

Instructions: You are the consultant in this situation, an employee of the state department of health. You are considered to be an expert on organizing referral services for troubled employees and on getting alcoholics into treatment.

You feel that this client organization is moving right along. It is a medium-sized manufacturing organization with six hundred employees in this plant, which is one of many similar plants around the country.

In this conversation, you are talking with the assistant personnel director, who is your primary internal contact. The assistant director has been supportive of the idea of developing a broad-brush identification and referral program for the troubled employee and has facilitated your consultation and training work in the plant during your last seven visits.

The purpose of this meeting is to **review what has developed so far, and to make plans for the future. You particularly want to end this interview with definite plans for what will happen during your next visit.**

During your past visits, you have done the following:

- Met with the director of personnel and the plant manager.
- Met with the assistant personnel director and established a working relationship.
- Initiated a series of workshops for educating supervisors on identifying the troubled employee and using referral resources in the community.

During the present visit, you have completed a round of training workshops with supervisors.
Your analysis suggests several things that should be done next:

- Meet with the union leaders to see how they are reacting to the program.
- Meet with a group of middle management people (directors of accounting, maintenance, shipping, manufacturing, sales, etc.) to help them examine what they can do to further the program.
- Meet with the medical and clinic people in the plant because you have not done this yet.
- Bring the director of the local rehabilitation clinic to visit the plant with you.

You would prefer to combine the last two items as your activity next time, but you want to check this out with the assistant personnel director before committing any dates.

Part 7. The Training of Consultants   205

OBSERVER'S GUIDE

Instructions: Several dilemmas are built into this situation and part of your task is to help your team mates to analyze, after the interview, how they handled the dilemmas. Please observe and take notes for the following:

1. Each person in the interview has his or her own idea about urgent next business. How do they present their ideas and organize them to make a plan?

2. The assistant personnel director is somewhat insecure in this relationship. Does the consultant sense this? What, if anything, does the consultant do about it?

3. The assistant personnel director wants individual service for the personnel director's spouse, but the consultant is taught not to give such special service. How do they handle this?

4. How clearly do the client and the consultant understand the plan for the next visit? Check this out and also elicit how they feel toward each other at the end of the interview.

Part eight
Management and Organization Development

44 Introduction to Organization Diagnosis

Purposes

I. To introduce managers to an interesting approach to organization diagnosis.
II. To identify organizational issues in preparation for problem solving.
III. To use a diagnostic instrument as a means of team building.

Group Size

This activity can be used with participants from a single organization or with a large audience by dividing them into small groups of five to eight persons each for discussion.

Time Required

One hour.

Setting

This instrument can be employed in a number of settings in which the concept of organization development (OD), and particularly the idea of diagnosis of organizational issues, is being introduced. For example, it has been used:

A. With a management team of a small organization of ninety employees as an introduction to OD.
B. As an activity during a lecture on OD to a large audience of managers.
C. As a device for collecting data from a group of thirty subordinate employees during the diagnostic phase of OD in an organization of four hundred employees.
D. As an activity for use by a management team in the absence of an outside consultant six months after the consultant had engaged them in an initial round of diagnosis, problem solving, and team building.

Materials

I. A pencil and a copy of the Diagnostic Window for each participant.
II. A blank flipchart, markers, and masking tape.

Procedure

I. Introduce the activity with comments that touch on the following points:

A. The identification of organizational issues that interfere with productivity is an important initial phase of organization development (OD).
B. Not all issues are amenable to change, some are easier to work through than others, and it is difficult to know where to start.

C. Change efforts are best expended where the likelihood of payoff is the highest. How can one sort out the variety of issues and choose those that can be worked on first?

II. Hand out a copy of the Diagnostic Window and a pencil to each participant.
Note: large audiences can be divided into small groups at this point; people should be placed with others from their own organizations wherever possible.

III. Explain the Diagnostic Window as follows:

A. In any organization it is possible to identify things that are working and things that are not — represented in the diagram in the vertical columns.

B. It is also possible to say whether these things are amenable to change or not — this can be indicated in the rows of the diagram.

C. Therefore, the upper-left quadrant is the healthy *Operational* aspect of the organization. It represents things that are working and, since they are amenable to change, they can be corrected if they get out of line.

D. The lower-left quadrant, called *Temporary*, represents things that are working but are not amenable to change. They are called temporary because they tend to slip up or sideways in the Diagnostic Window, becoming either better or worse without anyone doing much about them. Examples include: a key person who is not productive but who will retire soon; an office that has to be located in a temporary building; or a group of new employees who are not doing as well as they might but who may become better by on-the-job experience.

E. The lower-right quadrant represents the *Disaster Area*. These are things that are not working and are not amenable to change. Examples include: an incompetent employee who is in a high office of the organization for political reasons; a lack of a personnel policy manual; or runaway expenses for a product line that is not selling. These items must sometimes get worse before they can get better. They may be issues that have never been brought to the attention of the right decision-maker, or for which the time is not right for change.

F. The upper-right quadrant is the hopeful area. Things here are not working but they are amenable to change. This is the area of *Potential*, the field for organization development efforts. Since they can be changed, items in this area cry out for problem solving, for taking action so that they can be moved into the upper-left quadrant as things that are working. Many more organizational issues fall into this area than people usually realize, and an organized attack on them is called for.

IV. Assign the task to the participants as follows:

A. Think about your own organization and be as specific as possible as you fill in the squares of your diagnostic window. You may think of people, resources, the physical plant, the work environment, the mission, the organizational structure, intergroup relationships, the organizational climate, etc. But in the windows of the square identify the various "things" clearly rather than with general titles.

B. You have fifteen minutes to make your entries and then we will have a general sharing of them.

V. Place four sheets of flipchart paper up on the wall, one sheet for each quadrant. Label them:
- Operational
- Temporary
- Disaster Area
- Potential

VI. After fifteen minutes, ask members for their entries and write them on the large sheets so that the collective thinking of the group can be seen. (If this is done with a large audience of strangers, they may report first to the other members of their small groups. The experience ends with reports from each group on its ideas of elements that belong in a more formal organizational diagnosis.)

VII. Engage the group in a discussion. This usually becomes a form of team-building activity as members clarify their entries for one another, find areas of agreement in the placement of their items, and test the degree of hopefulness or discouragement concerning the ability of the organization to change.

VIII. Focus finally on the sheet that is labeled Potential.
   A. Ask the group to identify action steps they plan to take that can lead to change with these issues.
   B. It may be necessary for the group to: meet again for problem solving on these issues; hire an outside consultant; collect more data; form task forces.
   C. The meeting should end with a clear idea of the action steps that will be taken next on the items of the Potential area.

DIAGNOSTIC WINDOW

	Things that are working	Things that are not working
Amenable to change		
Not amenable to change		

From Steven Ruma, "A Diagnostic Model for Organizational Change," in Social Change, 1974, 4(4), pp. 3-5. Reproduced by special permission of NTL Institute for Applied Behavioral Science.

45 Win/Lose Competition

Purposes

I. To place people in a situation in which their side either wins or loses.

II. To examine the behavioral and effective consequences of a win/lose situation.

Group Size

Two groups of fifteen or fewer persons.

Time Required

Two hours.

Setting

A separate room for each group to plan in and a large room for the presentations.

Materials

I. A table of numerous prop materials, similar to those found in a theatrical storeroom, e.g., crepe paper, bells, musical instruments, fabric, costumes (masks, boots, old army jackets, hats), sheets of cardboard, fingerpaint, etc. The greater the quantity and mass of materials, the more weight and credibility will be given to the serious intent of the activity.

II. A copy of the Observer's Guide for the observer in each group.

III. A pencil and paper for two ballots for each participant.

Procedure

I. At the beginning of the activity, separate the two groups by asking members to sit together, so that the composition of each group is clearly identifiable. The groups may be intact training groups or task-force teams that have worked together and have developed some team spirit and sense of group loyalty.

II. Without identifying the win/lose aspect of the activity, give the following instructions:

   A. For the next couple of hours, we are going to have a competition between these two groups. Your task will be to prepare a five-minute presentation depicting how you may re-enter your daily lives back home most effectively and put to use your learnings from this workshop. (Alternative tasks: Depict learnings from this workshop; caricature the trainers.)

   B. The presentation may take the form of a skit, role play, singing commercial, or any form you wish. A supply of props is available for you to use. The presentations will be judged on the criteria of meaningfulness, originality, and skill of presentation.

C. We need one person from each group to serve as an observer. Who will it be? (Hand out a copy of the Observer's Guide to each observer.)
D. Before you begin to do your planning, we want to collect some judgments from you. Look at the make-up of the two groups. One of these groups is going to win. One will come out on top with a superior presentation. Considering the talent and drive of the people in each group, which one will win? (Hand out a pencil and a paper ballot to each participant.)

III. Collect the ballots, being sure that those from each group are identified and kept separate.
IV. Assign the groups to their planning rooms and tell them to work for forty-five minutes.
V. During the groups' planning period, tally the ballots and record the results on a flipchart in a form similar to the following:

    Group A: 12 members total   Group B: 11 members total
               10 voted for Group A   11 voted for Group B
               2 voted for Group B

                     Group B wins with 13 votes

Keep this flipchart page concealed until the second balloting is completed after the presentations.

VI. During the groups' planning, arrange the large room with a space for a "stage" at one end and the groups to be seated separately when they return.
VII. After forty-five minutes, have the groups return and give their presentations.
VIII. Ask the participants to pair across groups for judging the presentations. Hand out a paper ballot and instruct each pair to discuss the presentations in terms of the criteria: meaningfulness, originality, and skill of presentation. Then they will divide one hundred points between the two presentations with Group A rated first. The scoring could be 60-40, 35-65, 50-50, or the like.
IX. Allow about twenty minutes for the pairs to reach a decision. Collect the ballots and, with the participants watching, record the tally on the flipchart as follows:

Group A	Group B
60	40
35	65
etc.	etc.
Total	Total

(Group with the highest total wins.)

X. Uncover the flipchart sheet showing the results of the preliminary balloting and compare the two sets of results.

XI. Ask the observers to assist in processing the activity with focus on the following questions:
  A. What are the present feelings of the losing group? Of the winning group? Are these characteristic of a win/lose situation?
  B. How much did loyalty bind you during the preliminary balloting?
  C. What do the observers have to report regarding evidence of competition, rivalry, loyalty, and other we/they phenomena?
  D. What resemblance do these feelings and behaviors bear to real-life situations of competition and win/lose outcomes?

OBSERVER'S GUIDE

Instructions: It has not been announced to the groups, but an important aspect of this activity is to experience what it is like to be in a win/lose situation. One side will win by being judged "better," while the other side will lose. Competition tends to create this dynamic, and it has an effect on the attitudes and behavior of the participants. Your task is to observe for such effects.

Take note of evidence that the dynamics listed below are operating. They may become visible in individual or group behavior, in decisions that the group makes, in comments made by individuals, and in the level of drive exhibited. Continue your observations during the presentations and the final judging. It is during these times that feelings will especially be exhibited. Here are some cue words to guide your observations:

- Group loyalty
- We/they
- Feelings of success/defeat
- Feelings toward the other group
- Conflicts experienced:
  due to a desire to win
  due to loyalty to own group
- Resentment toward trainers for creating this situation
- Behaviors when the groups return to the large room
- Behaviors during the presentations

46 Volunteering

Purposes

I. To demonstrate how old habits and attitudes can prevent an individual from reaching out for new life experiences.

II. To assess individual tendencies toward risk-taking behavior.

Group Size

With a large audience, this is an excellent activity for demonstrating experiential learning. It also works well with a group of ten persons.

Time Required

About fifteen minutes.

Materials

A blank flipchart and markers.

Procedure

I. Announce to the group, "We are going to perform an experiment that will be fun to do, but I need five volunteers to come up here to help me."

II. Wait for a show of hands. Usually one or two participants will soon raise their hands, and their offer should be accepted, but ask them to remain in their seats until five volunteers have been obtained. Do not initiate the selection of anyone, but wait and watch expectantly until five persons have raised their hands.

III. When five persons have volunteered, say, "OK, that is the end of the experiment!" Ask members of the audience to take the next few minutes to talk with the people sitting next to them about the following points:

- Why did you, or did you not, volunteer?
- Do you feel positive or negative when asked to take a risk?

IV. Allow three to five minutes for the discussion, then conduct a general discussion covering the following points:

- Ask the others for a sample of reasons why they did not volunteer.
- On a flipchart, list the reasons for not volunteering.
- Ask whether these reasons are valid for all situations, and do they tend to interfere with participation in new and possibly rewarding experiences.

- Suggest that breaking down reticence can lead to a richer life, such as:

    Talking with a stranger
    Displaying one's ideas or feelings in a group
    Taking responsibility for an office in an organization

V. Summarize the experiential nature of this activity. It has consisted of an experience that included some heightened emotionality, an opportunity to engage interpersonally with others, a review of what happened, and a generalization to other areas of life.

47 Seven Questions

Purposes

I. To encourage feedback in a group during a training program.

II. To enable a staff that has an ongoing working relationship to provide feedback and to clarify the relationship patterns.

Group Size

Nine to twelve people who are fairly well acquainted with one another.

Time Required

One hour.

Materials

I. A blank flipchart, masking tape, and markers.

II. Paper and pencil for each participant.

Procedure

I. Introduce the activity by commenting on the need to know how the members of the group are beginning to perceive one another.

II. Hand out paper and a pencil to each participant. Ask the participants to answer each of the following questions by writing the name of someone in the group (display the questions on the flipchart):

Whom in this group would you choose . . .

1. To send on an important mission?
2. To discuss a new idea with?
3. As a companion for recreation
4. To ask for help if you were in serious trouble?
5. To be marooned with on a tropical island?
6. To escort your spouse across the country?
7. For a boss? (optional for an intact staff group)

III. While the participants are writing their choices, post seven flipchart sheets, one for each question, around the room. Label them BOSS, IMPORTANT MISSION, and so on. As the participants finish, ask them to enter their choices on the sheets, listing their own names on the left, then drawing an arrow from left to right, where they list the names of their choices.

IV. Allow time for all the participants to look at the sheets to see where their own names appear and what patterns develop for others in the group.

V. Lead the group into a discussion, covering the following points:
- What are the bases for certain choices?
- Why do some names show up more on one list than on others?
- Why are some people not chosen at all?
- Do any mutual choices appear?
- Is there any attraction of opposites? Of like-minded?
- Does this suggest things we might do to improve the way we work together?

48 Decision Making: An Unexpected Activity

Purposes

I. To experience a real-life example of group decision making.
II. To compare the real-life process with text-book examples.
III. To perceive the difficulties of introducing newly learned concepts into ongoing behavior.

Group Size

Five to seven participants per group.

Time Required

Thirty minutes.

Setting

Circles of chairs in a room large enough for the groups to talk without one group overhearing another.

Materials

A sealed envelope containing a question slip for each group which reads:

How did you decide to stop?
How do you feel about the way you reached this decision?

Procedure

I. Choose a time for this activity thirty minutes before a coffee break or before adjournment at the end of an afternoon.
II. Divide the participants into small groups. Using the flipchart, quickly review some of the methods by which groups reach a decision, such as the following:

The Plop: Your suggestion is ignored.

Railroading: A loud suggestion is acted on without discussion.

Self-Authorized Decision: You act immediately on your own suggestion; the group goes along.

Handclasp: Quick agreement between two people moves the group to follow their suggestion.

Voting: A tally of opinions is taken for and against a suggestion.

Trading: "I will agree with you on this one, if you will go along with me on the next."

Consensus: Everyone expresses willingness to go along, after having a chance to contribute his or her individual opinion.

III. Give an envelope to each group and say:

> Before we break, will you take a short time to identify examples of any of these decision-making methods that you recall from our experience today. When you are ready, you may leave, but before leaving, open this envelope and read what is inside.

IV. At a later point in the program, offer the following questions for discussion:
  A. What feelings were associated with the various ways you reached your decision?
  B. When would it be appropriate for a group to adopt an authoritative method of decision making? A collaborative method? Consensus?
  C. What difficulties are you apt to find in trying to improve the way a back-home group reaches its decisions?

49 Team Building: Disposing of the Past

Purposes

I. To allow for expression of "the good old days" by a management team.

II. To recreate the rapid growth recently experienced by the team.

III. To dispose of the past and start anew with the present team.

Group Size

An intact management team of nine to twelve persons.

Time Required

One hour or more.

Setting

This is a special event for use with a management team that has experienced rapid growth in a relatively short time, say, in two to four years. This is not an unusual circumstance in agencies, such as mental health centers or other communication organizations, that have received an infusion of governmental funds. It is also true of organizations that have experienced a major reorganization.

A distinctive feature of rapid growth in a group is the split between the old guard and the newcomers. An effective vehicle is needed for mourning the passing of the carefree intimacy of old and for valuing the rewards of having a new organization that can accomplish new goals. The newcomers need to feel that they are legitimately and truly a part of the group. This activity works well as a change from the intensive problem solving that characterizes a team-building session for such a group.

Materials

I. A sheet of blank flipchart paper and markers.

II. Wine and cheese for all the participants.

Procedure

I. At an appropriate time, often after a brief evening work session on the first day, express the observation that the group is really made up of two subgroups, the old guard and the newcomers. Check out this feeling with the group members and identify the persons in each subgroup.

II. Ask the old guard members to sit at the table and the others to draw back, sitting around them and well out of the focus of their attention.

III. Place a sheet of flipchart paper and markers on the table and encourage the members who are sitting there to doodle during their conversation.

IV. Ask the group at the table to talk about the old days:

> How was it then?
> What did you like about the way you operated and related to one another?

V. Allow the old guard to reminisce for about fifteen minutes and then ask, "Who was the first new person to join you?" Ask that person to sit in with them at the table as they continue to talk. Gradually add each new member to the group in the order in which they joined the organization.

VI. You probably will need to do very little to maintain the flow of recollections and feelings. When the group is all reassembled, if they have not covered the following items, you might ask:

   A. As you joined the group at the table, were you treated in the same manner as when you came on board in the organization (ignored, not made room for, not looked at)?
   B. Is it more difficult to keep track of people now, with so many at the table, than when the group was smaller?

VII. At this point, move in and say:

> This paper and its art work represents the former organization. (Begin to fold up the sheet of flipchart paper and continue to do so while talking.) It no longer represents anything that is real. I'm going to remove it, with all due respect, and put it where it will no longer interfere with your working together. It will be cared for, but you do not need it any longer.

Silently fold the sheet into as small a packet as possible and take it from the room. It should be placed where no member will see it again, even by chance.

VIII. Allow the group to continue with its conversation for a considerable length of time, then return and sit in the background.

IX. After a short period, offer the wine and cheese and say, "Let's celebrate the team we have here now."

50 Team Building

Purposes

I. To provide a condensed experience in team building.
II. To develop a theory of the process of team building.

Group Size

Participants work in groups of six. Any number of groups may be included, but there should be an even number of groups for pairing.

Time Required

Two hours.

Setting

A large room in which the groups are visible to one another but do not interfere with one another's work.

Materials

A sheet of flipchart paper, masking tape, and a marker for each group.

Procedure

I. Ask the participants to seat themselves in circles of six persons each and to strive for a heterogeneous mix of age, sex, race, and occupational background in each group.
II. Introduce the activity with the following comments:

We are going to have an experience with team building. I will give you some topics to discuss in your small groups. Each topic will be in the form of an incomplete sentence. You can use the sentence as a jumping-off point for a discussion, and each discussion period will last for only seven or eight minutes. The object of discussing these topics is to help you to draw close to one another as you would if you were working as a team over a long period of time. I apologize for the times when I will be interrupting your conversation, but we must keep this moving along. The first topic is:

When I first enter a new group, I feel . . .

III. Monitor the groups carefully to determine whether they are working on the topic as assigned and whether they have discussed as much as they can on the topic. They should be urged to *discuss* the topic rather than merely going around the circle for brief individual completions of the sentence.

IV. After six or seven minutes, interrupt the group discussion and announce the next topic. Follow the same procedure for four more topics selected from the following list:
- On my job, my greatest strength is . . . (*brag about yourself*)
- A personal weakness in me, and something I am trying to improve, is . . .
- When I was ten years old, I . . .
- I usually try to make people think I am . . . (*what is your facade?*)
- The person I love most of all is like . . . (*not "who" but what is he/she like?*)
- In this group, my impression of each of you is . . . (*make sure that each person gets some feedback*). (*Note: a longer time is necessary for this topic.*)

V. Ask the groups to pair together all around the room. Give no directions as to how they are to do this. Simply say, "Groups A and B will sit together and Groups C and D will sit together, etc."

VI. When they are seated, say, "Now look around you at this new group. Do you feel differently than you just did in the other group?" Wait for a spontaneous nodding of heads or comments. Then say, "If I were to give you a personal topic to discuss, would you be as able and willing to go into it?" Again, wait for a few comments, then say, "Something happened back in that other group to change it from a collection of people to something more like what we mean by the words *group* and *team*. Go back to your small group and talk about this. What did you do, or what happened, that formed you into a *group?*"

VII. Before the discussion begins, distribute a marker and a sheet of flipchart paper to each group and ask that someone record the group's ideas for later sharing.

VIII. After about ten minutes, ask the groups to share their ideas. As each group reports, post its sheet of flipchart paper at the front of the room. The sheets usually will include content areas from the discussion topics, and other things such as "having eye contact," "touching," and "laughing together."

IX. Summarize by pointing out that the topics were chosen to increase openness among team members by:
- Sharing feelings in the here and now
- Learning about one another's jobs
- Learning about strengths and weaknesses
- Getting some personal background in depth
- Getting and giving feedback

Point out how many of the ideas they shared in step VIII are similar. In effect they have generated their own theory of team building.

X. Optional Step: The teams formed in this way can be used effectively for later small-group work in the training program. In addition, if there is time, they can discuss their experience with teams back home such as a committee, office staff, or task force. Which of the elements here are present in those teams? If some elements are lacking, does their absence have an effect on the way the people work together?